ALTARS
of
POWER *and* GRACE

CREATE THE LIFE YOU DESIRE

ACHIEVE HARMONY, HEALTH, FULFILLMENT, AND PROSPERITY
WITH PERSONAL ALTARS BASED ON VASTU SHASTRA

By

ROBIN AND MICHAEL MASTRO

Balanced Books

We dedicate this book to our children, Anna and Mike, for their enthusiasm and encouragement, and Amy, for her amazing insight and support.

It is our true desire that this book opens you to the sacred in everyday life and brings with it blessings of peace, harmony, and grace.

ALTARS of POWER and GRACE

Create the Life You Desire

By Robin and Michael Mastro

© 2004 Robin and Michael Mastro

Published by:

Balanced Books

P.O. Box 14957

Seattle, WA 98144

www.balancedbookspub.com

All rights reserved

Editorial and Production: Andrea Hurst

Layout and Design: Insight Design (www.insightdesign.org)

Production Manager: Usana Shadday

Book Design and Layout: Ian Szymkowiak & Alan Hebel

Photography:

Dave Monley

Angie Norwood Browne

Remy Haynes

Scott Hague

Harry Haugen

Peter Chelsom

Library of Congress Control Number: 2003116921

Publisher's Cataloging-in-Publication

Second Printing

Mastro, Robin.

Altars of power and grace : create the life you
desire through the sacred art of vastu shastra /
by Robin and Michael Mastro. – 1st ed.

    p. cm.

    LCCN 2003116921

    ISBN 0-9749109-0-2

1. Vastu. 2. Hindu altars. I. Mastro, Michael.
   II. Title.

BF1779.V38M37 2003   133.3'33

                          QB104-700051

First Edition

ISBN: 0-9749109-0-2

Printed in Singapore

Acknowledgments

This book was a true labor of love and a demonstration of trust in the Divine process. We would sincerely like to acknowledge our editor and friend, Andrea Hurst, for her untiring commitment and vision. Her vast experience in the field of publishing has been invaluable. We also wish to thank Cummings Walker, Lisa Siegel, Linda McClenahan, Mai Tran, Christina Lutman, Sandy Althen, and Elizabeth Monley for helping us with the birthing of this book. Your support and dedication in seeing this vision become a reality is so very appreciated. A special thanks goes to Justin Hurst for conceiving the design of the cover. To our design team at Insight Design, Usana Shadday, Ian Szymkowiak, and Alan Hebel: thank you for creating such a beautiful book. To Fei Chen, thank you for going that extra mile and helping us with printing. We would also like to thank our photographers, who worked on many different phases of the book: Dave Monley, Angie Norwood Browne, Remy Haynes, Scott Hague, Harry Haugen, and Peter Chelsom. Each of you was able to show the beauty of the altars in your own way. An added thanks to Scott Hague for designing some of the yantras presented in the book.

We want to thank our friends John Thompson at Illumination Arts and Royce Richardson at Ancient River Publishing for sharing their knowledge of the publishing industry with us. A special thank you to Peter and Camille Stranger, Brenda and Rob Spears, Dean Thompson, and David Rothmiller, our very dear friends, for their wisdom, knowledge, and friendship. We'd also like to thank DiVanna VaDree, Danielle Becker, Gwenn Henkel, all of our friends, both local and international, through the Art of Living Foundation, as well as our students and clients who cheered us on and have been our greatest supporters.

Special thanks go to Farouk Seif, Core Faculty, Whole Systems Design, Antioch University, who inspired me to open myself to the process of discovery and seek the road less traveled. To Sri Sri Ravi Shankar, our dear friend and spiritual teacher, for his unconditional love and support of our work worldwide and for showing us the Divinity that resides within.

We want to thank our parents for their encouragement and support. We know how the creation of this book took us away from you during the final process of writing, editing, and completion. We appreciate your patience and love.

And finally to the guides, angels, gods, and goddesses who support us in so many ways. We are eternally grateful for your grace.

TABLE OF CONTENTS

SECTION THREE: Resources

CHAPTER 1

Altars of Power and Grace : The Evolution

Since the dawn of civilization people have created altars and shrines in sacred places where they invoked the spirits, prayed to their deities, and expressed their devotion to the mysterious forces that guided their lives. In the Western world, shrines were memorials erected in homes or at wayside crossings to commemorate saints and ancestors and to honor the dead. Altars, where spiritual ceremonies took place, were usually found in churches and temples. The services and rituals performed in these places were considered the province of established religions. In recent years, the idea of having private altars has gained increasing popularity.

In this book are innovative steps, based on the ancient science of Vastu Shastra, to create empowering and transformational altars. These altars are designed as sacred spaces where you can ask for Divine inspiration, for grace to infuse your life, and for help to make your dreams come true. This system was developed over several years of extensive study of both Feng Shui, the ancient Chinese art of placement, and Vastu Shastra, the primary system of sacred architecture used in India for more than seven thousand years.

For many years my husband, Michael Mastro, and I have taught yoga, meditation, and other spiritual awareness techniques as part of the Art of Living Foundation, a nonprofit, humanitarian organization whose purpose is service to humanity. Michael, a meditator for more than thirty-five years, traveled extensively with the renowned spiritual teacher, Maharishi Mahesh Yogi.

> "These altars are designed as a sacred space where you can ask for Divine inspiration and grace to infuse your life and help make your dreams come true."

During the last thirty years, Michael has become one of the leading Western experts on the art and science of Vastu Shastra. In the mid-1970s, as a graduate architecture student, Michael was asked by the Maharishi to design spiritual centers in India, Europe, and the United States using the principles of Vastu Shastra. He then began to apply this ancient Vedic system of placement in his work to build and create living environments in harmony with nature, including using the science to determine the environmental orientation of the first Microsoft building.

Although Vastu Shastra had enormous appeal to me, I felt it was too complex and difficult for Westerners to integrate into their busy lives. However, I also knew that the benefits offered by this system, to harmonious-align our personal space with the powerful energies of the Universe, were too important to set aside.

I decided to find a way to simplify the complexities and to extract the most potent aspects of Vastu Shastra. I knew there were tangible benefits in this ancient art that would point the way to an evolving system adaptable to the realities of today's world.

At that time, I was completing a graduate degree at Antioch University in the new field of Whole Systems Design, which, simply stated, teaches how to think systemically, operate holistically, and design creatively. We had also purchased a home that conformed to the general outline recommended by Vastu Shastra and were busy remodeling it in accordance with Vastu principles.

After we moved in, our lives changed dramatically. Our health improved, our family relationships blossomed, and our finances improved – even our pets benefited from the change. I was convinced of the great advantages the system offered.

Shortly after moving into our home, we were invited to travel throughout India with the founder of the Art of Living Foundation, Sri Sri Ravi Shankar. Wherever we went in India we saw altars: they were placed at roadside rests, in people's homes, and in meditation halls. The Divine seemed ever-present in this culture. Ceremony and common daily rituals went hand in hand. Altars provided a tangible connection with the Divine apparent, and this was the essential piece I had been looking for to define my graduate work. I had gone to India knowing

that Vastu would be the subject of my graduate project, but I hadn't known how a system derived from it would emerge. I thought perhaps the answer was to create small areas in a home or office where these principles could be incorporated, even if they could not be applied throughout the dwelling. From listening to peoples' concerns about how to integrate Vastu, I knew it needed to be not only aesthetically appealing but also simple enough to understand and powerful enough to impact their lives.

Upon returning home I developed a model for creating altars based on Vastu and incorporated it into my graduate work. Along with my husband, I worked on the design, taking into account directional influences and the placement of each of the five elements to create the results that were inherent in the science itself. Anyone could assemble such altars in their homes or offices, whether or not their environment fulfilled the requirements of this ancient system.

This book teaches you how to create dynamic altars based on principles of Vastu Shastra as seen through the lens of Whole Systems Design. Michael and I have taught classes and worked with clients for several years to create altars based on this new understanding of an ancient art. Reports from people who have assembled altars have been outstanding, and in some cases truly amazing. In this book we present examples of altars to demonstrate different ways they can be coordinated with various decors and lifestyles.

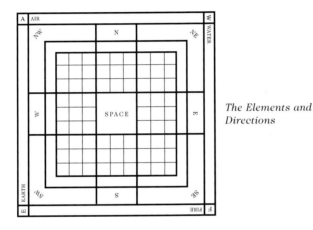

The Elements and Directions

We believe, and our experience has demonstrated, that by following the simple directions presented here, anyone can create altars that attract spiritual empowerment and manifest positive results. I hope that you will find the inspiration in this book to create your own altars — altars which please you aesthetically, open you to Divine energy, and help you to attain the desires of your heart.

"Wisdom begins in **wonder.**" —Socrates

CHAPTER 2

Vastu Shastra: The Science and History

The unique system used in this book to design altars was developed during our several years of study and practice in the ancient science of Vastu Shastra. This sacred teaching has been used in India for more than seven thousand years. Through our studies and research we found it to be a dependable, consistently successful system producing reliable results.

Keeping the Science Simple

Vastu Shastra has influenced peoples' lives in India for thousands of years. It presents guidelines for arranging environments in specific ways so they will be in proper alignment with cosmic energies. But remodeling your home or moving your furniture to live up to an ideal arrangement may not be practical. We all tend to get discouraged when faced with impossible demands. Still, ancient systems have much to offer. The altars you create with the system presented in this book can influence your environment in ways very similar to making larger changes. One thing is definite: you will begin to see changes occur in your life, changes that are fulfilling and supportive.

The scholars and architects of ancient times who developed Vastu Shastra were intimately acquainted with natural forces: the progression of the stars through the sky, Earth's magnetic fields and thermal energies, the relationships between land and water, hills and valleys, compass directions, and even astrological charts. Over the centuries subtle connections between these forces and the well-being of people came to be understood. This knowledge was carried from India to

Items for a Relationship Altar

China by Buddhist monks and was adapted to the Chinese culture and region. There it became known as Feng Shui.

The architects who helped evolve the system of Vastu Shastra were aware that living and working environments profoundly affect people. They learned to build homes and places of work and worship that harmonized with the cosmic flow and insured that people would benefit from good health, happiness, and prosperity. Solar energy, the pull of the magnetic poles, relationships to bodies of water, and other factors were taken into consideration when planning buildings so they would not only be functional but would also attract beneficial spiritual energy.

Because of the great value these ancient Eastern systems of architectural placement can contribute to modern homes and offices, these teachings are being reexamined and used extensively in our world today.

Yoga is also based on the Vedic wisdom texts of India. It fosters a healthy body and mind, and can help us experience life more attuned to the natural world. In the same way that yoga helps us balance the physical and spiritual energies of our bodies, Vastu Shastra balances the energy of our living environment. According to a

renowned Vastu architect of Madras, India, Dr. V. Ganapati Sthapati, every inch of the earth is in perfect cosmic order. We believe that adhering to Vastu principles, even on a small altar, brings power and grace to wherever you live or work.

Altars of Power and Grace, which is based on principles of Vastu Shastra as seen through the lens of Whole Systems Design, offers a basic plan that can be adapted to any belief system and features a wide variety of items, religious or otherwise. Any altar based on the Vastu system presented in this book is a dynamic, transformational tool that will empower you to achieve what you most want in life. Based on our research and our clients' positive experiences, we have found this system not only easy to follow but also the most successful method for manifesting your heart's desires.

Parvati

The World Through Ancient Eyes

Both schools of thought, Vastu Shastra and the field of Whole Systems Design, agree that all life is explicitly connected. We are not separate from our natural environment; everything is a part of the whole. Vastu Shastra teaches that we are influenced by solar, lunar, and magnetic energy, as well as by the five elements. We all know living things require the sun for growth. Light is essential for our wellness and enhances the function of our physiology and psychological outlook. Scientific research has shown us that the different rays of the sun impact our bodies in different ways — some are beneficial and others have been determined to be harmful.

> "Vastu Shastra balances the energy of our living environment."

The ancient scholars, *rishis* in Sanskrit, knew the rays of the morning sun supplied the most beneficial light of the day and were vital to the human body for good health. We call this light ultraviolet. They were aware that as the sun moved directly over head it became more intense, producing rays which could be harmful to the human body. We know these rays as infrared. They also knew that as the sun continued to move toward sunset, the rays it produced caused disturbances in cellular activity. We call these gamma rays.

These sages could see how the moon influenced the waters upon the earth and in our bodies. Many people are aware of how their moods change right around the full moon. Statistics show more accidents, births, and deaths occur around this time as well. The moon impacts us in overt and subtle ways.

These sages also observed the effect of the magnetic earth energy on our physiology and emotions. Since our blood contains iron, we are shaped by the magnetic forces of the earth which can directly influence our lives.

The Five Elements

The concept of the five elements is the foundation of the science of Vastu Shastra. Everything in the Universe and in all of nature, including our physical bodies, is made up of the five elements. When we balance these elements using the principles of Vastu, which we do when creating an altar, we energetically make a system which filters out non-supportive energy while allowing helpful, life-enhancing energy to pass through. Once your altar is in place, it will resonate with natural forces and invite the spiritual help you need.

> "When creating an altar, we energetically make a system which filters out non-supportive energy while allowing helpful, life-enhancing energy to pass through."

"The most beautiful thing
we can experience is the
mysterious."

—Albert Einstein

CHAPTER 3

Our Desires, Aspirations, and Dreams:
Introduction to Creating Altars

The ancient sages believed that basic human desires, or aspirations, fall into eight general categories. When we build altars based on Vastu Shastra, we place them in the specific areas of a room, home, or office which correspond to what we want to change or enhance in our lives. For example, if you want to create prosperity in your life, you would build an Abundance and Prosperity Altar in the north. Or, you might be interested in developing a spiritual connection with the Divine. You would then build a Spirituality Altar in the northeast. The categories below correspond to the eight directions. Each direction carries within it specific influences that will profoundly affect the success of your altar.

The Eight Directions and Their Corresponding Aspirations

ASPIRATION	DIRECTION
Abundance and Prosperity	North
Spirituality	Northeast
Health and Well-Being	East
Life Changes and Transformation	Southeast
Career and Recognition	South
Helpful People and Universal Support	Southwest
Creativity and Knowledge	West
Relationships and Marriage	Northwest

Career Altar

The Significance of the Directions

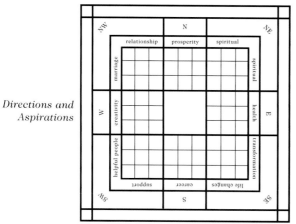

Directions and Aspirations

Vastu Shastra assigns meaning to the directions based on the movement of the sun across the sky from east to west and the magnetic influence of the north-south poles. Magnetic energy runs from north to south. Solar energy runs from east to west. These two forces create a solar magnetic grid that covers the earth and affects every inch of the planet.

1. Abundance and Prosperity — Abundance and prosperity are supported in the north. On the surface, the energy is quiet with deep magnetic currents running below. The quality of light is least intense in this direction, but most constant. The consistent quality of northern light provides ongoing nourishment and support.

2. Personal Spiritual Work — Personal spiritual work and our connection to spiritual knowledge are most supported in the northeast predawn energy. This light is the most powerful of the day. The intense quality of light disorients the mind, illuminating the soul. In this sector, the water element is at home.

3. Good Health and Well-Being — Good health and well-being are aligned with the rising sun in the east. This light promotes growth through its ultraviolet rays. It is considered the most beneficial and life-promoting light of the day.

4. Life Changes and Transformation — Life changes and transformation occur in the southeast where the light radiates more intense energy and creates greater heat. Here we surrender our thoughts and take our deepest concerns to be transformed at the doorway of the great Unknown. The fire element is at home in the southeast.

5. Career and Recognition — Career and recognition are illuminated in the south, as the sun is at its highest point shining directly like a spotlight. The sun is overhead in its most intense stage in this direction. This bright, illuminating energy attracts acknowledgment from the world.

6. Helpful People and Universal Support — Helpful people and Universal support assist you as the sun is descending in the afternoon sky, touching the ground. In the southwest, the sun's energy is a sustaining and grounding force, allowing relationships that nurture and encourage our growth. The earth element is at home in the southwest.

7. Creativity and Knowledge — Creativity and knowledge are gained as the sun sets in the west at the end of the day. The activity of the day is subsiding, and work is replaced with time for nurturing the soul through creative endeavors and learning.

8. Relationships and Marriage — Relationships and marriage are enhanced in the northwest sector where the sun is replaced with lunar influences. The northwest is associated with the element air, or wind, which encourages communication in existing relationships and attraction between people.

> *Magnetic energy runs from north to south. Solar energy runs from east to west.*

The Influence of Color

Altars are directionally placed, associated with the aspirations mentioned above, and contain the five elements represented in a specific order. The following diagram is your "roadmap" to manifesting your heart's desires. You will find how color influences the efficacy of the altars.

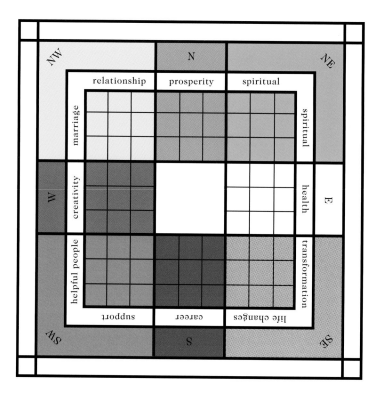

As you can see on the chart above, we recommend setting up altars that coincide with the eight aspirations. Each aspiration has its natural place on the diagram of the eight directions, with specific corresponding colors that heighten its effect.

The colors associated with the directions vibrate at specific frequencies, which complement the desires of each direction. The effect is similar to a radio being properly tuned to a particular station. In the radio, the crystal component vibrates at the same rate as the broadcasting frequency of the station, making it come in clearly. Using color helps stimulate the intention of your altar. For example, white encompasses all colors. It is the fastest wavelength and it positively affects the healing process. We use it as the primary color on a Health and Well-Being Altar. We assign primary and secondary colors on all altars. The secondary col-

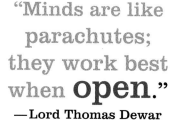

"Minds are like parachutes; they work best when **open**."

—**Lord Thomas Dewar**

or can be used as an enhancement. These colors should be represented on your altar but do not need to be the only colors used.

1. A Prosperity and Abundance Altar should go in the north sector of your home, preferably on a north wall or even a north windowsill. Primary color, green; secondary color, gold.

2. Your altar asking for spiritual knowledge belongs in the northeast area of your home. Primary color, gold; secondary color, white.

3. For assistance with health and well-being, place your altar in the east. Primary color, white; secondary color, gold.

4. To request support in life changes and transformation, your altar would go in the southeast. Primary color, silver; secondary color, red.

5. Place your Career and Recognition Altar on the south wall. Primary color, red; secondary color, gold.

6. An altar dedicated to support from helpful people goes in the southwest. Primary color, orange; secondary color, red.

7. Your altar asking for assistance with creative projects and knowledge goes in the west. Primary color, blue; secondary color, yellow.

8. An altar inviting personal relationships or grace for your marriage goes in the northwest. Primary color, yellow; secondary color, blue.

Suggestions for necessary and optional items and instructions for the positioning of each of the elements to maximize the potency of your altar are discussed in the next chapter.

CHAPTER 4

Representing the Five Elements:
Items to Use and Their Placement

The Elements

Each altar you create will have items made from or associated with the elements of earth, air, fire, and water. It should also have an offering related to the space element and a Personal Symbol.

Items representing each element will go in the quadrant of your altar where its natural energy resonates with the cosmic forces:

AIR in the northwest

WATER in the northeast

EARTH in the southwest

FIRE in the southeast

Your offering goes in the middle, in the area of akasha (or space, in Sanskrit), where a vortex has been created by the correct placement of the elements. A Personal Symbol of the result you are hoping for goes in the back, behind the offering. Please follow these diagrams carefully. The arrangement of items on your altar is important if you wish to benefit from the power of Vastu Shastra.

When selecting items to place on your altar, you have the opportunity to be as creative as you wish. The most important thing is that your altar must touch your heart. It is from that place of resonance that the alchemy of transformation occurs. Through the energy of love, you create a dynamic system that feeds the altar, which in turn supports the fulfillment of your desires.

Creating the Space

You may want to define the space for your altar with an attractive piece of fabric, a beautiful scarf, or some other material that complements your creation. This is more a matter of personal taste than a required component of the altar itself.

The air element distributes seeds of blessings and good wishes.

The list below gives you general suggestions for items you might use.

Air Element In the northwest air quadrant, you might use feathers, flags, miniature kites, angel or bird figurines, or anything else that floats in the air. Fans, chimes, bells, flutes, or other objects that create sound waves carried by the air are also wonderful choices. Incense, which wafts through the air, can also be used in this corner. The air element distributes seeds of blessings and good wishes. Our hopes and dreams move through the air to the Supreme Presence to be fulfilled.

Water Element Use water in any container in the northeast quadrant. Water represents our emotions and our desires. Pure water symbolizes our sincere intention aligned with our highest good. You can float petals on the water, or use a vase of water with flowers in it. Some people who design altars recommend using a transparent container so the water can be seen. A fountain or fishbowl might be a good choice for you. If you use fresh flowers, don't let them turn brown or die. Silk flowers are fine if you have water in the container. Dried flowers should be avoided. You want your flowers to be as alive as your dreams.

Earth Element The earth element is the grounding force that gives birth to possibilities. You can use rocks, metal or ceramic statues, natural crystals or stones, items made of wood, or anything taken from the ground. Plants or seeds that germinate and bring new life can represent new opportunities coming into fruition.

Fire Element Candles are the most popular choice, though an oil lamp or aromatherapy lamp would be fine. Incense represents fire as well as air, so you can use incense here,

The finest riches of health wealth and happiness are constantly blossoming in my life.

also. Fire brings passion to your manifestation. It has the ability to create or destroy, depending on the intention. It is the element that can transform raw desire into fulfillment.

Offering Tray In the middle of the altar place an open bowl or dish, or any flat object that can hold within it a symbol of your intention. For instance, you can write out your desire on a piece of unlined paper. It can be as simple as one word, such as "abundance," or you can expand it into an entire affirmation. Some of my favorite affirmations include thoughts about what I desire most: love, abundance, good health, and fulfilling relationships. They should be personal and simple, such as "The Divine supports my abundance in all ways," or "Joy and peace flow to me from the Grace of the Universe." Angel Cards® are a popular choice – they have a picture of a tiny angel on them and one word such as "love." If you like, you can use something other than words to symbolize your desire, such as coins or jewelry for prosperity, or seed pods for growth.

Many of our clients add yantras to their offering tray or dish to give the altar an added boost. A yantra is a geometric pattern. The designs were created thousands of years ago and were encoded with sacred sounds. Included within the design are the vibrations of the five elements. Yantras transmit powerful frequencies and hold cosmic energy that enhances our lives on every level of existence. There are many different designs of yantras, each one having a specific influence on the environment.

Karla Siddhi Yantra

When yantras are added to the Offering Tray or placed anywhere on an altar, its potency is increased. Throughout the altar chapters, individual yantras will be discussed.

Personal Symbol In back of your offering tray, place a picture or other item that represents the result you are hoping for. If you want a new house, find a picture of your dream home, frame it beautifully, and place it in this position. Some people use statues or sculptures of people or deities that represent a particular quality to them. Many people create collages from pictures they have on hand. My favorite family altar has a collage of photos of my parents, my daughter, my husband, and other family members with big smiles on their faces. Every time I see this altar, it touches my heart and reminds me of the good times we've shared. I send up a tiny prayer that all of our days will be filled with joy.

> " Your sacred items may be statues or pictures of deities, gods, and goddesses from the world religions, old and new. "

Touching Your Spirit

Virtually everyone who attends our altar workshops uses items on their altars that are in some way sacred to them. These can be personal mementos collected over a lifetime or something found that touched your heart. The items can be religious in nature, like a menorah or a rosary. They can be representations of people who have influ-

Relationship Altar

enced you and have shown you through their actions and attitudes that they are worthy to admire and hold in a position of honor. Your sacred items may be statues or pictures of deities, gods, and goddesses from the world religions, old and new.

Strictly speaking the altars do not require a statue of Buddha, a picture of Christ, or any other representation of a spiritual leader in order to attract Grace and power. But many people want to ask for the blessings of their favorite saints, angels, gods or goddesses, and don't feel that their altars are complete without them. Often, we see altars with more than one spiritual guide watching over them, as well as other items, like pressed flowers from a wedding bouquet or a hand-written recipe from a mother, that have touched the heart and spirit.

One of our favorites is a lovely Relationship Altar built to attract a soulmate. It includes a graceful statue of Kuan Yin, the Chinese goddess of compassion, and a lovely picture of the Virgin Mary. Both represent grace, love, and power to Amanda, the creator of the

altar. Amanda is devoted to both Mary and Kuan Yin, and to the love they represent. Every time she passes her altar or goes there to pray or meditate, she immediately feels love in her heart. An altar that engenders positive feelings is always the most effective.

At our house we have a whole pantheon of Hindu gods and goddesses to choose from. Dearest to me is Lakshmi, the goddess of abundance. I have several little statues of Lakshmi and use them on my Abundance Altar and other altars as well. Having an abundance of health, joy, and creative ideas makes sense to me.

Lakshmi

You will see a great variety of personal mementos, sacred religious objects, gods, goddesses, saints, holy men and women, gurus, and other links to the Divine pictured on altars throughout this book. Please feel free to borrow ideas if they feel right to you, or supply your own spiritual inspiration. Like different paths that lead up a mountain, we believe that all spiritual paths lead to the Power that Creates All Things. *See Appendix II for a list of gods and goddesses.*

The Most Important Element

Though it doesn't show up on the diagram, the most important thing you can place on your altar is your own emotion, for it has great power. Try to select items you love to look at, that give you a lift when you see them, and that engender hope and joy in your heart whenever you pass by. Imagine how you will feel when your dreams begin to come true, when your heart's longings begin to manifest in your life. Your little altar is meant to speak to your soul as well as to your Higher Power. Your own positive emotions are a strong bridge to the world of spirit and will help you gain what it is you wish for. Personal experience has taught us that it is advisable to begin slowly and create a maximum of two altars at a time. Desire has power and change will occur. It is best to see what transpires from your first one or two altars before creating more.

"The future belongs to those who believe in the beauty of their **dreams.**"

—Eleanor Roosevelt

CHAPTER 5

The Process of Manifesting Your Dreams and Desires

The Universe overflows with Grace. We have only to focus our minds and hearts, clearly state our needs, and send our requests to the Divine. The Universal Presence always responds, though sometimes in surprising ways. You may be shown new options or given information about what is blocking you. An altar is a microcosm of our larger universe in perfect order, without obstruction and with all five elements in balance. When this perfect balance exists, there is nothing to oppose your desire becoming manifest.

Igniting Your Altar

Altars nourish the longings of your heart. Even if you have only a few minutes, you can go to them anytime to pray, meditate, and reaffirm your intentions. Altars turn your rooms into sacred spaces and remind you to keep your heart open and your spiritual lines of communication well tuned.

Create Room for Unlimited Possibility

It is advisable before initiating the process of creating an altar to take time to make your environment as clean and clutter-free as possible. Placing your attention on clearing unnecessary items, on cleaning and organizing your home or office, sends an important message to the Universe that you are ready for change and are taking responsibility by clearing the way. You might notice in the process of cleaning and clearing that memories and old thoughts, even regrets, will surface. Each time you feel some emotion that tends to bind your mind to a feeling of regret or disappointment, *stop* and notice where this sensation is in your body. You might feel it as an ache or an emptiness in a specific region. Once you have a sense of where it is, take a deep breath in and, as you exhale, make the sound "Ahhh," just like the sound you might use when, on a hot summer day, you take a much-needed drink of cool, fresh water. This is an ancient sound that will move any negative energy that weighs heavily within your body, replacing it with a feeling of relief and freedom.

In this process of clearing out old, outdated, or unwanted objects and items, you are releasing that which does not serve you any longer. In doing so, a burden will be lifted. The physical objects in your surroundings that you no longer need or use weigh you down. Letting go of unwanted or unnecessary things frees up your personal energy and stimulates the creative force within you.

Preparing Your Altar

Once you have cleared out those things that hold your energy to past thoughts and activities, you are ready to begin.

- Use a compass to identify the proper direction or area for the altar.

- Place your altar in the area or sector of your home or office associated with the aspiration you desire to manifest in your life. It can be put on a table, counter, cabinet, windowsill, or any available space.

- Remove any dirt or dust from the area with a clean cloth.

- If you desire, you can use a tray, a piece of fabric, or other material to create the space on which your altar will sit.

- Select the items you will be using on your altar to represent each of the five elements. Look for objects you already have at home before going out to buy something new. Adding or replacing objects on your altar is always fun to do. Good places to look for altar items are garage sales, thrift stores, Asian grocery stores, health food stores, and home stores. *See Appendix.*

- Use items that touch your heart, that you find beautiful, or that have meaning to you.

- Place the items representing earth, air, water, fire, and space (akasha) in their proper directions.

- Add other items to create the feeling you want, once the five elements have been represented.

- You must be able to see the water. If you use a vase, make sure it is transparent. A fountain is also a good choice. It is fine to use a small, flat dish or bowl where the water is visible. Always use purified or filtered water.

- Add your Personal Symbol.

- Before beginning your ceremony, shower and put on fresh, clean clothes.

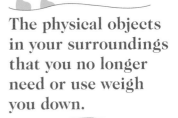

The physical objects in your surroundings that you no longer need or use weigh you down.

When using the science of Vastu Shastra, an altar is set up in a square or rectangular shape. Remember, the water element is in the northeast, the fire element is in the southeast, the earth element is in the southwest, and the air element is in the northwest. The space element is in the center of the altar, and your Personal Symbol is just behind the space element. Once these items are in place, you can decorate your altar with added pieces that bring you a feeling of beauty and harmony.

Being in the Flow – The Importance of Gratitude

Being grateful for what you have in the present moment is the first law of manifestation. Gratitude is the elixir that the Universe cannot ignore. This is an important piece to recognize, especially when creating altars. If you reside in a place of gratefulness, more will be given to you. Be willing to ask with an open heart in order to allow your dreams to manifest. Gratitude is essential for the success of your altar. When you remain open, without impatience, your altar will become an irresistible magnet that will draw the intention of your Spirit into form.

It is best not to be too specific in your requests to the Divine, as it will limit the possibilities of that which might be for your highest good. If you come to your altar with commands and demands, it will impede the flow of opportunity. If you feel doubtful, critical, or skeptical while creating your altar, these feelings will impact it and dilute its success. It would be better in this instance to wait until you are more open and receptive to begin this process.

We Possess Great Power

There is a powerful force that is available to everyone, yet it is unused or misunderstood by many. The power that resides within each of us can be expressed through prayer, the spoken word, meditation, and intention. It is capable of influencing our reality. It is said that the unlimited power and grace that resides within the Universe answers every one of our prayers, every longing, all of our wants, and all of our desires. All these requests can come back to us fulfilled. But, sometimes we make it more difficult by our doubts and feelings of unworthiness. Because of our lack of clarity or our inability to allow ourselves to be in the flow of manifestation, the yearnings of our soul may appear to go unanswered.

Our thoughts, words, and beliefs impact the way we perceive our daily lives in both positive and negative ways. Imagine for a moment that our external Universe has an innate flexibility and is shaped by our thoughts and beliefs and the influence of our perceptions. Whatever we put our attention on will grow, whether it is positive or negative. It is our challenge and our mastery to *keep our attention on our intention:* not in an overt and obsessive way but through the cultivation and nurturing of our connection to the unbounded presence of the Divine. It is in the subtle field of Infinite Consciousness that true power and grace manifest. Through this doorway, created by your altars and the ceremonies you perform, transformation occurs.

Bringing Intention into Form

Your altar is just a gathering of treasured objects until you bring it to life with prayer or ritual. Move things around until you are satisfied with how it looks, paying special attention to the original layout as your guideline. After you have finished creating the altar, it is time to make your request to the Divine so that which is unseen, yet permeates all that is, understands your intention. Doing this will empower and enliven your altar. We suggest that less is more here. This is not the place for pages of specifically spelled-out longings, but a distillation of the end feeling or desire to be represented. Better to feel the sense of wonder and fulfillment as you go about igniting your altar than to limit the results by being too specific.

Here are a few suggestions that might inspire you.

> ▪ Write one word or several words that will evoke an emotional response (i.e. happiness, love, health) on a piece of unlined paper that will fit nicely in your Offering Tray.
>
> ▪ Find one or more small objects that symbolically represent the feeling you desire to experience and place them on your Offering Tray.
>
> ▪ You can add items that inspire you, such as Tarot Cards or Medicine Cards with symbols that resonate with you. You can also place a yantra, or write a mantra on an unlined piece of paper, that calls forth the experience you are looking to receive. A technique for igniting your altar, using yantras and mantras, can be found in each of the individual altar chapters.

Once you have placed your written words or symbols into the Offering Tray, stand or kneel in front of your altar and clear your mind by taking some long, deep, slow breaths in and out through the nose several times. With your eyes closed, feel the presence of the altar in front of you. There is a power building there. You can sense it even before it is activated. By gathering together representations of the five elements and your treasured mementoes, you have designed a physical representation of your intention. Your altar is filled with possibilities and holds within it your hopes and dreams.

If you have incense on the altar, it is time to burn it. If you have a candle placed there, light it. If there is a bell or chimes on the altar, ring them. If you have a fountain on your altar, make sure it is working well.

ACTIVATION TECHNIQUES FOR IGNITING ALTARS

Once you have completed the above steps, there are several ways to activate your altar. You may already have a preferred ceremony or technique. If you do not, below are some suggestions that you may resonate with.

Yantras and Their Corresponding Mantras

Within each altar chapter, a very powerful technique is offered using a specific yantra and corresponding mantra. Yantras are powerful physical representations of an intention or influence. The yantras we offer in this book are specific and emit an energetic field that affects the aspiration associated with the direction in which it is placed.

As a gift to our readers, we have created a special page on our website, www.vastucreations.com/freeyantras, on which you can download an appropriate yantra for the altar you are creating.

Whenever you use a yantra for activating your altar, there is a corresponding mantra to be chanted or repeated out loud to complete this particular activation process. A mantra is a sound that purifies the environment and impacts the five elements. Everything in the Universe is made up of the elements of earth, air, fire, water, and space. Mantras are powerful, ancient words in Sanskrit that move Universal Energy in specific patterns, uniting the mind and heart. They create a resonance that allows manifestation to occur. Combined with the appropriate yantra, mantras profoundly influence the environment, bringing harmony, balance, and support.

Prayer as a Portal to Power and Grace

Prayer is a wonderful way to create dialogue with Divine Consciousness. This consciousness permeates all that is known and unknown. This consciousness is in relationship with us, whether we are aware of it or not. Genuine prayer comes from a willingness to let go of agendas, expectations, and outcomes, and to ask with heartfelt humility for the peace, fulfillment, and support that we all desire to experience. This process is done once your altar is set up and your candles and/or incense lit, bells rung, etc. With all your heart and with deep longing, create a sincere inner dialogue with the Divine Presence. Turn within and open yourself to this intelligence and consciousness. Ask for grace to be given to you, and you will be answered.

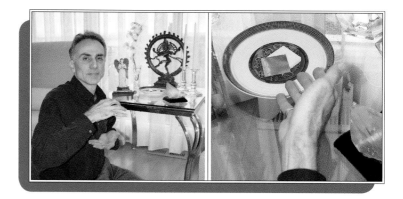

A Ritual for Manifestation with the Energy Ball Technique

This is a powerful technique for infusing your altar with energy by creating an energy vortex using the breath, and physically drawing energy, creating a power-ball to ignite your altar. Here is how you proceed:

- Stand or kneel in front of the altar and clear your mind. Bring your awareness to the feelings you would like to experience, the purpose for creating this altar.

- Have your left hand in front of you with palm up at chest level.

- Take a deep breath in and, as you do, bring your right arm straight up, palm extended toward the sky. As you slowly exhale, bring your right hand down toward the left palm, creating an imaginary ball.

- Repeat this process three times. You will feel the energy build each time you bring your right hand down toward your left hand, creating an energy ball.

- After the third time, transfer the ball into your right hand and place this created energetic ball over the top of your offering tray.

- You have ignited your altar.

A Ritual for Manifestation with a Keystone

The ancient Vedic design etched on the Keystone was configured thousands of years ago and is a very auspicious symbol. Used properly, it guarantees protection and positive results in all undertakings. The Keystone is hand-carved in carefully chosen marble that contains the highest crystal content, allowing it to embody your personal aspirations and intentions. The design of this symbol has been created for specific purposes; one use is to ignite altars. Before they are sold, an ancient ceremony of preparation and purification is performed on them, charging them to add to their potency.

A Keystone has an amazing ability to turn the altar on. Below is the process to ignite an altar using the Keystone.

1. Hold the Keystone to your heart in your right hand, covered by your left hand.

2. Close your eyes and take some long, slow, cleansing breaths in and out through the nose.

3. Imagine how wonderful it would feel to have what it is you desire.

4. Build those feelings within your heart until your heart is overflowing with this sensation. Then imagine you are transferring the fullness of these feelings to the Keystone.

5. When you have completed this transmission, place the Keystone in front of the Offering Tray, centered between the two elements in the front, or you can place it on the Offering Tray itself.

Tending Your Altar

Your altar immediately begins to transmit the frequency of your desire, once it is ignited. The items placed on the altar create an energy grid where Divine intention is brought into three-dimensional form. Like any living thing, your creation needs tending. You can pray, meditate, chant, sing, or just sit in front of your altar and admire it.

Feed your altar with appreciation. Do this by making sure there is fresh water and flowers, if you have used them. Keep the altar and the objects on it clean of dust and dirt. Replace objects that have lost their significance or no longer feel in harmony with your intended results. By maintaining your altar, you support its potential and the work that it will do for you. Just as giving positive reinforcement to a child reaps long-term rewards, giving to your altar of your time, attention, and love will support its on-going success in your life.

If for any reason you feel your altar is beginning to lag or not produce the benefits you would like to enjoy, take everything off the altar and begin the process once again. Be patient and know that you have created a very potent connection with the Divine Source where all things become manifest.

> Just as giving positive reinforcement to a child reaps long-term rewards, giving to your altar of your time, attention, and love will support its on-going success in your life.

"Everything in nature contains all the power of nature. Everything is made of one hidden stuff."

—Ralph Waldo Emerson

SECTION 2

The Altars of Power and Grace

INTRODUCTION

The next eight chapters are based on the eight aspirations.

They feature pictures of altars and give directions for creating them. Each chapter contains a layout for an altar; a yantra with its associated mantra that can be used to ignite the altar; and a table of correspondences for each aspiration, including colors to use, powerful days of the week, spiritual guides that watch over each specific area, special metals associated with each altar, the aroma that best supports your intention, and other elements that empower the altars.

The system presented in this book will guide you in creating altars for your home or office, to attain your desires and fulfill your destiny. You will also learn about altars for special occasions and one for World Peace.

I hope the altars in this book inspire you to create your own. Start with just one or two and see what happens. I change my altars around frequently to suit my ongoing hopes and my family's needs. I tend mine as though they are living things that need care and feeding.

Think of your little altar as a doorway to the unseen. Every time you give it attention, it becomes activated, and the door to divine grace opens a little wider.

"Grace brings forth knowledge."

—Sri Sri Ravi Shankar

CHAPTER

Altars that Invite Abundance

hat does abundance mean to you? What would you do if you knew you would always have more than enough? What would it feel like to be confident that your needs would always be met? Imagine if you had a beloved, extremely wealthy uncle, and you were his favorite and accepted heir. Just for a minute take a deep breath in, and as you let it go feel what it is like to know you will be taken care of, that you will never again need to worry about having enough. Did you feel something shift inside?

The tendency of the mind is not to believe, but deep inside, beyond the doubting mind, there is something that says, "Yes! This feels good and I like it!" Don't we all want to be light hearted and joyful, happy to be alive? When you live in abundance, that's how you feel.

The experience of abundance is very personal. To you, it might mean enjoying your inner wealth, spiritual riches, or a life overflowing with happiness. It could mean having a new home, plenty of money, a cornucopia of creative ideas, a full roster of clients, or a bulging portfolio.

The Flow of Abundance

We created an Abundance Altar at our house at a time when we were waiting for three large checks to come in. Following the traditional Vastu Shastra principle that a constant, supportive flow of positive energy associated with prosperity comes from the north, we placed our Abundance Altar against a west wall in the north sector of our home at the top of the stairway, with the intention of encouraging wealth to flow in our direction.

Space was limited, so I used a tiny antique end table for a base and placed small objects on the altar. Though our intention was great, we sought the limitless abundance of the Universe. The stairway proved to be a wonderful location. Each time we went up or downstairs, we were reminded to say a little prayer inviting abundant grace to flow into our lives. The altar felt very cheerful and lighthearted to me, just the qualities that I experience when I'm feeling prosperous. In fact, I liked the altar so much that I found myself running upstairs to visit it during the day. Within a week the Universe accepted our invitation – all three checks came in.

"
The altar gives us the comfort needed to feel aligned with the Universal Energies of abundance.
"

THE PLACEMENT

Air: A small golden fan in the far right (northwest) quadrant of the altar.

Water: A translucent green vase containing ivy cuttings in the front right sector (northeast). Flowing water symbolizes the abundant flow of prosperity, so a fountain or small bubbler would have been a good choice had there been enough space.

Earth: A statue of Lakshmi, Hindu goddess of abundance, on the left quadrant of the altar (southwest).

Fire: A green candle in a pale green soy sauce dish on the front left (southeast) corner.

Personal Symbol: A design with dollar bills framed in gold. I stood the frame on a beautiful carved green box a friend had given us. Gifts subtly remind us how nice it is to receive.

Offering Tray: A slip of paper that says *Abundance* placed in a green porcelain dish at the center of the altar. Also added is an abundance necklace of my design, with a pendant that displays a planetary yantra and stones that relate to this direction.

Additional Items: A potted, flowering plant.

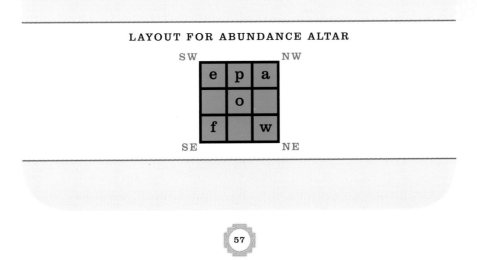

LAYOUT FOR ABUNDANCE ALTAR

SUGGESTIONS FOR YOUR
ABUNDANCE ALTAR

- Make sure the area is clean and your surface is against a northern wall or window, or in the north sector of your home or office.

- The colors gold and green should be used in some pieces on this altar.

- The water element in the northeast can be fresh flowers in colors that correspond to the altar. You can use a vase that is clear or lightly colored.

- Use a green or gold candle in the southeast, or an oil lamp.

- Use stones or crystals in the southwest in green or golden colors. You can use a statue of Lakshmi, the goddess of abundance, a plant, or anything from nature.

- For the air element in the northwest, use a standing wind chime, incense, a fan, or a feather.

- You can hang a green-colored Austrian leaded crystal on a red string in increments of nine inches over the center of your altar to keep the abundance you desire moving in your direction.

- Add a dish or small plate in the center of your altar to act as a place for your offering. Use gold or green.

- You can add a Shree Lakshmi Yantra to your offering dish for an extra boost of positive energy, or a Ganapati (Ganesh) Yantra to remove all obstacles to your abundance.

- On an unlined piece of paper that can easily fit onto the Offering Tray, add a handwritten word, an Angel Card®, or some other symbolic representation of the abundant feeling you would like to receive from the Divine.

- Include a Personal Symbol in the center, in back of the offering tray of your altar. It can be a statue, photograph, collage, or picture that inspires feelings of abundance.

Activation Ceremony
Creating Abundance and Prosperity Using the Mercury Yantra and Mantra

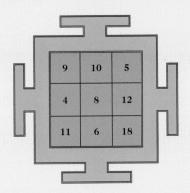

Each direction has a unique influence and a specific planet associated with it. The planet Mercury influences prosperity and abundance and is associated with the north. If desired, you can use the specific directional yantra for Mercury that can be seen in the diagram above. You can sketch or trace your own version of the yantra, or for a free downloadable version you can go to our website at *www.vastucreations. com/freeyantras*. Other activation processes can be found in Chapter Five. On the following page is the activation process for your Abundance and Prosperity Altar, using the Mercury Yantra and its corresponding mantra.

THE ACTIVATION CEREMONY

▓ Stand or kneel in front of your altar.

▓ Light any candle or incense that is on your altar.

▓ If you have bells or chimes on your altar, ring them to purify the energy in the environment. Their sound resonates with higher, subtle vibrations, bringing focused awareness to the present moment.

▓ Holding the Mercury Yantra in your right hand, take ten to twelve long, slow, deep breaths in and out through the nose.

▓ Experience the feeling of having what you desire. Do not focus on specifics, just feelings like happiness, peacefulness, fulfillment, love, and so forth.

▓ Place the yantra on the Offering Tray.

▓ Using your right hand, extend the small (pinky) finger and your index finger, folding in the other two fingers against your palm, placing your thumb over the top of these two fingers to hold them in place. This is a mudra, in Sanskrit, a hand position that moves energy in a specific pattern.

▓ With your hand in this mudra, facing the altar, move your arm forward and back nine times.

▓ Each time you extend your arm toward your altar, say the following mantra with passion and intensity:
Mantra: *Om Budhaye Namaha*
Phonetic Pronunciation: Om Boo-da-hay Na-ma-haa

▓ Once you have completed this process, your altar is ignited.

▓ Take time each day to acknowledge your altar, even in small ways. This stimulates and keeps it activated.

CORRESPONDENCES FOR ABUNDANCE AND PROSPERITY ALTAR

PRIMARY COLOR	*Green*
SECONDARY COLOR	*Gold*
QUALITY	*Abundance*
AROMA	*Peppermint*
GEMSTONE	*Emerald, malachite, jade, and other green or golden colored stones*
METAL	*Silver, gold*
HINDU DEITIES	*Lakshmi, goddess of wealth; Ganesh, remover of obstacles*
YANTRA	*Shree Yantra**
MANTRA	*Om Maha Lakshmaya Namaha*
OTHER SPIRITUAL MENTORS	*Fortuna, Abundantia*
PERSONAL SACRED ITEMS	*Gold coins, richly decorated fabric, photographs*
SPECIAL PEOPLE	*Benefactors who represent generosity and support*
DAY OF THE WEEK	*Wednesday*
SOLAR SYSTEM	*Mercury*
ANIMAL	*Elephant*
LORDS OF THE DIRECTIONS	*Kubera*
ELEMENT	*Air and Water*
PLANT	*Basil*
SENSE	*N/A*
SHAPE	*N/A*

*The Shree Yantra (with corresponding mantra) can be added to your Offering Tray or used as a separate or additional yantra to ignite your altar.

Altar for a Family in Transition

Elena loved the feeling of her new home as she walked through the rooms. She had created a sanctuary for herself and her two daughters. With the sudden death of her husband, her life had been in turmoil for over a year. Finally, she felt that she was in a place of healing, which brought her a sense of peace. She was more aware than ever of her desire to insure the continuous flow of abundant universal support for their growing needs. She didn't want to feel overwhelmed by the financial demands that were hers to bear alone. She knew if she could create a deep connection to the Divine, it would bring them financial security and free up her mind to focus on the future in a more constructive way.

Her budget was limited, so Elena visited an import store in her neighborhood to look for some items for her altar. There she found a stunning statue of Lakshmi, the goddess of wealth and prosperity, both material and spiritual, as well as other pieces to add to her altar. Back home she rummaged through unopened boxes in the attic which had been given to her by an aunt who had traveled extensively, and here she found everything else needed. She designed a beautiful little altar on a small table and placed it in front of a north window.

Elena called me to come and take a look at her creation. I added a Shree Yantra to the Offering Tray, and together we ignited the altar with a Keystone. Elena's altar is a wonderful example of putting together something beautiful, meaningful, and powerful for very little money. She lights her candle and meditates daily, focusing on her intention. The altar has given her the comfort she needs to feel aligned with the universal energies of abundance.

Items for an Abundance Altar

Feeling Prosperous in an Overwhelming World

Beth, an account executive for a radio station in New York City, assembled a Prosperity Altar in her office early in the year. It was a simple altar with just the basic items on it. She used Deepak Chopra's book *Creating Affluence* as her personal symbol for prosperity. Beth and a friend did a little prayer ritual to activate the altar. In February she called with good news.

"I've been in advertising for years. We usually have a slump right after the first of the year, but not this year. The phone kept ringing off the wall. It actually started the morning after we did the ritual. I can't remember a time when we've had more new clients come in out of nowhere. So far, it's been the busiest winter we've ever experienced!"

The Divine Answers

A Seattle doctor, Caroline, mentioned at one of my classes that during her youth in Europe she had created a small altar of her own. Then, after the class, she assembled a Prosperity Altar in her home. She later said, "As I was putting it together, I felt connected to God. Creating my sacred space became a sacred act. It was lovely." A week later, out of the blue, a friend from France called and offered to invest in a clinic Caroline plans to set up.

Various pieces for an Abundance Altar

"You see things as they are and ask, 'Why?' I dream things as they never were and ask, 'Why not?'"

—George Bernard Shaw

Your Journey Awaits

As with any of the altars in this book, the process of creating an Abundance Altar will set in motion a remarkable journey of self-discovery. As you consciously co-create your reality with the Source of All That Is, you will begin to realize your true nature and unlimited potential. Always remember to be patient and to remain open as this process unfolds.

CHAPTER 7

Altars to Support or Draw Relationships and Marriage

There is nothing more important in the world than love. Love is the nectar that sustains and nurtures us. It is the sweetness and joy that comes from a heart filled with lightness and appreciation. Within each of us is the essence of love. Sometimes you see it when you look into the eyes of babies or young children. It is as if they open their hearts to you in recognition. Other times it appears as a radiant light glowing in the eyes of the elderly. They may have learned from a lifetime of happiness and sorrow that within each moment is the opportunity to celebrate love. In those special moments, know that the spark you see in others is also within you. At your very core, love is all you are.

To feel love and be loved is a sincere blessing. What does love mean to you? Is it a deeper relationship with yourself or perhaps a feeling of strong connection with the grace and power of Universal Acceptance? Maybe what love means to you is giving your heart to another and having it genuinely received with acceptance. It might mean diving into unknown depths of tenderness and allowing yourself to surrender in an already existing relationship. Whatever form of love you wish to enhance or manifest in your life, a Relationship Altar will be your ally in supporting your heart's desires and will help you cultivate a deeper understanding of who you are.

A Heart's Longing

Jerri had a great life, good friends, and a wonderful job that fulfilled her desire for creative work and opportunity for advancement. Her family was proud, life was full, yet Jerri's love life lacked luster. Inside her heart she knew she was ready for a mate. Being a warm and happy person, she had several male friends, but she wanted something deeper and she knew now was the right time.

When we spoke initially, I asked Jerri to describe a normal day and a normal week in her life. Next I asked her to step back and view her life as if it were somebody else's. What could she tell me about her life when looking at it from a different perspective? From this new viewpoint she realized there seemed to be no room for anything new to happen. Her life was a regime: get up, go to work, pick up groceries, go to the gym, grab dinner out, go to a movie with friends, watch TV, or shop.

Jerri realized from this exercise that she had insulated herself, lived a very predictable life, and had no space for new possibilities to occur. Every day was a routine that was comfortable and that guaranteed she would continue to feel success and pride in her work and life. But it wasn't enough for her heart, and she realized that in order to create a relationship that touched her deeply, she would need to risk some of the certainty and let down a few of her walls.

I gave her the directions for items to use on a Relationship Altar. Jerri spent the next few days during her lunch hour looking through some stores in town where she found wonderful pieces to place on her altar. She also looked in her storage room and on the shelves of her curio cabinet for additional mementos. She placed these items in their appropriate positions and invited me over to look at her creation and to instruct her on how to ignite the altar.

She had set up the altar in her study on a small table in the northwest corner. First she used a beautiful brocade cloth from India to define the area and then began creating her altar with her new purchases and treasured family pieces. For her air element in the northwest, she used a small standing wind chime with a heart symbol on it to represent the love that she felt inside. She was ready for that love to resonate in the world and attract a mate. She added a beautiful cut crystal vase in the northeast with fragrant blue lilacs in it, a scent she loved. Her fire element in the southeast was a small blue candle in a porcelain dish, and her earth element was a heart frame. Within the frame she chose a picture of Radha and Krishna, whose legend of love has been recounted throughout the ages. For her Personal Symbol, she added a statue of Parvati, the Mother Goddess, to remind her of the purity of her intention. She placed the statue on a beautiful blue velvet box — a family heirloom. Upon the small glass plate she used for her Offering Tray, she added a bright yellow seashell in the shape of a heart, an Angel Card® with the word *love* printed on in, some blue crystals, and blue lace agate beads as decoration. Her altar turned out to be a wonderful expression of beauty and love. She prayed in front of it daily, remembering the importance of taking time to create an ongoing dialogue with the Divine to help support her intention.

I heard from Jerri a few months later, and it seemed that her life had definitely taken a positive turn. She had begun seeing a nice young man, a friend of a business associate. She said that over their first dinner, she had felt something stirring inside that definitely caught her attention. That feeling had continued to grow, and her heart now felt tender and so very much alive. The deep yearning for something more and the ritual of creating the Relationship Altar and offering the Divine her heart's desires had opened her to the love she longed for. She was beginning a new journey filled with gratitude and joy.

THE PLACEMENT

Air: Small standing wind chimes placed in the far right (northwest) quadrant of the altar.

Water: A cut crystal vase with lilacs in the right front corner (northeast) of the altar.

Earth: A picture of Radha and Krishna in a gold frame, signifying devotional love, placed in the far left quadrant of the altar.

Fire: Blue candle placed in a blue and white porcelain dish in the front left (southeast) sector.

Personal Symbol: A statue of Parvati, the Mother Goddess.

Offering Tray: A small glass plate with a yellow heart seashell, an Angel Card®, blue crystals, and blue lace agate beads.

Additional Items: A blue velvet box on which Parvati, the Mother Goddess, is standing.

> **Remember to have the area on which you place your altar clean of dust or dirt.**

LAYOUT FOR THE RELATIONSHIP ALTAR

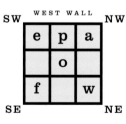

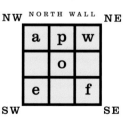

SUGGESTIONS FOR A RELATIONSHIP ALTAR

- Remember to have the area on which you place your altar clean of dust or dirt.

- The Relationship Altar is placed in the northwest area of your home or office, on a windowsill, wall, table, or other surface. It can be placed facing north or west, depending on your available space.

- The colors yellow and blue should be represented in some of the pieces of the altar.

- For the air element in the northwest, you can use chimes, feathers, incense, a bird figurine, an angel, a fan, or similar items.

- To energize your altar, you can hang a blue crystal on a red string in increments of nine inches above the Offering Tray.

- The water element in the northeast could be a cup or bowl of water, or a vase in one of the altar colors. The water needs to be visible, so if it is in a vase, make sure that it is translucent or clear. You can add fresh or silk flowers to the vase, as well.

- As the symbol for the earth element in the southwest, you could use a crystal, or stones such as blue lace agate, or pearls. Even a green plant or one with yellow or blue flowers would do nicely, an African Violet, for example.

- A candle in the southeast would be a good choice for the fire element. If you like to add fragrance, use one with ylang ylang. You can also use an oil lamp. Look for one that is silver in color, if possible.

- The Offering Tray can be in colors of yellow or blue, or made of silver colored metal or clear glass; whatever you use, make it a complementary addition to your altar.

- Your Personal Symbol in the center of the altar behind the Offering Tray might be a statue of Parvati, the Mother Goddess, who symbolizes goodness, purity, power, and strength. She represents Shakti, which is the supreme feminine energy or female power. Or you could use a statue of Krishna, who exemplifies loving relationships. You could also create a collage that evokes the experience you would like. It can be made of old photographs or even magazine clippings whose words, symbols, and pictures of people inspire you.

- If this altar is to encourage a new partner relationship or to enhance an existing one, add items in pairs. Two fish, two doves, two hearts, for example, are symbolic of successful relationships.

- For a boost of Cosmic Energy, add a Ganesh Yantra to your Offering Tray in order to remove all obstacles, or a Shree Karya Siddhi Yantra to bring about fulfillment of your desires. You can also add an appropriate Rune, Angel Card®, AltarCard®, or any other symbol, including gems or necklaces with the correct corresponding colors to infuse your altar with energy.

Activation Ceremony
Attracting Successful Relationships Using the Moon Yantra and Mantra

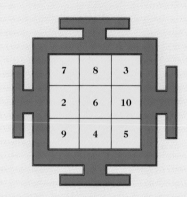

The influential planet corresponding to the energies of the northwest is the moon. It supports success in relationships and the stability of the mind. You can download a usable version of the appropriate directional yantra (Moon) by going to our website at *www.vastucreations.com/freeyantras*. This book offers several manifestation techniques to ignite your altar. For additional methods, other than the one offered on the next page, please go to Chapter Five. On the following page is the activation technique for your Relationship Altar, using the Moon Yantra and its corresponding mantra.

THE ACTIVATION CEREMONY

⚙ Stand or kneel in front of your altar.

⚙ Light any candle or incense that is on your altar. If you have bells or chimes on your altar, ring them to purify the energy in the environment. The sound of bells focuses the mind and illuminates the present moment.

⚙ Holding the Moon Yantra in your right hand, take ten to twelve long, slow, deep breaths in and out through the nose.

⚙ Experience the feeling of having what you desire. Do not focus on specifics, just feelings such as happiness, a sense of peace, fulfillment, love, and so forth.

⚙ Place the yantra on the Offering Tray.

⚙ Using your right hand, extend the small (pinky) finger and your index finger, folding the two middle fingers in against your palm. Place your thumb over the top of these two fingers to hold them in place.

⚙ With your hand in this mudra, facing the altar, move your arm forward and back nine times.

⚙ Each time you extend your arm toward your altar, you will say the following mantra with passion and intensity:
Mantra: *Om Chandraye Namaha*
Phonetic Pronunciation: Om Ch-on-drey Na-ma-haa

⚙ Once you have completed this process, your altar is ignited.

⚙ Remember to feed your altar with your love and appreciation. Doing so will positively influence your results.

CORRESPONDENCES
FOR THE RELATIONSHIP ALTAR

PRIMARY COLOR	*Yellow*
SECONDARY COLOR	*Blue*
QUALITY	*Change*
AROMA	*Ylang ylang*
GEMSTONE	*Pearl, moonstone, blue lace agate, or lemon quartz*
METAL	*Silver*
HINDU DEITIES	*Parvati, the Mother Goddess, Krishna*
YANTRA	*Ganesh Yantra**
MANTRA	*Om Gum Ganapataye Namaha* (pronounce Gum with an ng sound instead of an m)*
OTHER SPIRITUAL MENTORS	*St. Valentine, Archangel Gabriel, Eros, Luna, Hera*
PERSONAL SACRED ITEMS	*Pictures of people in happy relationships or objects that are symbolic of successful relationships to you*
SPECIAL PEOPLE	*Those who represent successful relationships that you admire*
DAY OF THE WEEK	*Monday*
SOLAR SYSTEM	*Moon*
ANIMAL	*Rat*
LORDS OF THE DIRECTIONS	*Vayu*
ELEMENT	*Air*
PLANT	*Eucalyptus*
SENSE	*Touch*
SHAPE	*Crescent*

*The Ganesh Yantra (with corresponding mantra) can be added to your Offering Tray or used as a separate or additional yantra to ignite your altar.

Loving Relations

To inspire a loving family relationship, we built an altar when all of our children were teenagers. They were ages nineteen, seventeen, and fourteen, and we were in the midst of uncharted territory, needing a sacred place to honor their process as well as our own. We wanted not only to be their parents but also life-long friends, and it was to this commitment in our hearts that we chose items that would evoke the deeper feelings we intended. We placed the altar on a small table in the northwest area of the house on a west wall. To remove any obstacles that could stand in the way of our relationship with them,

> As our Personal Symbol I made a lively collage containing several members of our family, putting our three children at the very top of the design, and framing it attractively.

we chose Ganesh, the elephant god who is considered the protector and lord of the journey, as our earth element. We used a clear crystal statue of Ganesh on a decorative stand in the southwest corner of the table. For the air element in the northwest, we placed a standing wind chime with the symbol of a heart on it. For water in the northeast, we used a low copper bowl with a yellow rose and three healthy ferns as symbols representing our children's gifts and beauty. We feel very lucky to have talented and creative children. For the fire element in the southeast we added in a clear glass container a yellow candle that was infused with the fragrance of ylang ylang, a scent related to the northwest that enhances the quality of relationships. For the space element we chose a beautiful hand-blown glass bowl that was my grandmother's. In it we placed an Angel Card®, printed with the word *tenderness* and added a carved terracotta heart. As our Personal Symbol I made a lively collage containing several members of our family, putting our three children at the very top of the design, and framing it attractively. For a design element, I added blue glass beads and scattered them on the table. To ignite the altar, we used the Moon Planetary Yantra, which is the directional yantra for the northwest.

Whenever we passed by the altar we would admire it and send love, knowing this action also stimulated its potency. For many years this Relationship Altar supported our desire to maintain loving family relationships during a very unique passage of time in our lives. Several years have passed since then, and our children are now young adults in their twenties, living their lives to the fullest. As their parents and friends, we are very proud of their achievements. More than this, we are touched by the people they have become: unique, productive individuals with open hearts and so much to give.

The Goddesses at Work

Goddesses for a Relationship Altar

Quan Yin and Mother Mary have always been special symbols of the love and grace of the Divine Feminine energy. One of our clients, Lindsey, felt they would be perfect allies on her Relationship Altar. She wanted a relationship where all that she was, her strengths and her weaknesses, would be accepted and appreciated. Tired of dating, she was looking for more than just someone to go out with. She wanted a union of heart and spirit. All the men she had known were either Sunday sports fanatics or too immersed in New Age rhetoric. She liked sports herself, but she wanted balance in her life. She wanted someone to share her pursuits and to grow spiritually and emotionally with her. He needed to be well-rounded and enjoy her love of nature and outdoor activities. It was with this in mind that she created her altar. She took time daily to sit in front of it, feeling her connection to the Goddesses that she knew were at work for her in the unseen. Within a month she met a man who matched many of her heart's desires. It amazed her that this simple process of requesting what she wanted and activating her connection with the Divine Feminine through the use of her altar could be so powerful.

Nichole's Story

Nichole was a beautiful, talented, and successful woman who hadn't had a date in three years. A graphic artist, she worked for herself at home and loved it. She had a full life with an amazing assortment of great women friends. It didn't seem right that such a vivacious and loving woman who would have liked to be in a relationship would be without the companionship she desired. Nichole and I created a little Relationship Altar in her garden window using pieces found around her home. When it came to a Personal Symbol, I suggested she look for a picture in a magazine of someone

Items for a Relationship Altar

that symbolized the feeling of the person she wanted in her life. Once she found a picture that touched her heart, she framed it and added it to the altar. She also added another picture of a couple she knew well whose almost-thirty-year marriage was still going strong. Within a week she had three men asking her out for dates. She chose the one with the sweet smile and kind-hearted ways.

Trust Faith and Remain Open

Loving support for your dreams and desires surrounds you. It is only by asking for what you want that the fulfillment of your heart's longings can ever be answered. It takes trust in the process you are undertaking, faith that you will be assisted along the way, and the willingness to remain open. The true magic begins when you reach out to the loving arms of the Unseen.

> It is only by asking for what you want that the fulfillment of your heart's longings can ever be answered.

"The moment you have in your heart this extraordinary thing called love and feel the depth, the delight, the ecstasy of it, you will discover that for you the world is transformed."

—J. Krishnamurti

CHAPTER 8

Altars for Enhancing Career and Recognition

How do you perceive career success and recognition? Could it be having your dream job? Maybe it is doing something that not only makes you happy but benefits others as well. Perhaps being recognized by your peers or having a corner office or a high salary equals success for you. Ultimately, we all want to feel fulfilled and acknowledged for the work we do.

Imagine for a moment that your profession brought you success, respect, and admiration for a job well done. Notice what it feels like when you visualize this. Do you feel a sense of expansion, or do you doubt this possibility? All of us, to varying degrees, have within us an aspect of self that I call the *disbeliever*. Its primary function is to maintain the status quo and limit your experience to what you already know, but it need not control your life forever. Creating an altar will help diminish the impact of the thoughts, beliefs, or limitations that stand in the way of having the success and recognition you desire. It will nurture your spirit and support your intentions for career expression.

A Celebration of Success

After finishing graduate school, I created a Career and Recognition Altar in our breakfast room. I wanted to acknowledge myself for the accomplishment of obtaining my masters degree in Whole Systems Design. I also wanted to fan the flames of inspiration to support and draw in my future success, and to use my multi-faceted educational skills as an integral part of my new work path.

This altar was built on minimal space against the south wall.

I wanted easy and consistent access, and the breakfast room seemed an excellent choice.

The selections I made for my altar were both meaningful and whimsical. Each piece was lovingly decided upon. In the process of creation, many items were chosen and then discarded before the altar was complete. I began with a wonderful picture of myself graduating as my Personal Symbol. In it my adviser, Farouk Seif, a PhD architect from Cairo, is placing the hood over my head, a symbol of achievement and completion. It was an expansive and exciting moment for me, one I will never forget. The picture represented the end of my

> These altars are designed as a sacred space where you can ask for Divine inspiration and grace to infuse your life and help make your dreams come true.

formal educational pursuit and a fresh beginning as I entered into the world of new ventures. Now was the time to manifest a meaningful avenue of expression using the unique skills and abilities I had acquired at school, and to craft my future work.

The picture set the groundwork for the rest of the objects on the altar. Since space was limited, for the air element in the northwest I chose a small bell a friend had brought me from India. For the water element in the northeast I used a petite, cut crystal perfume bottle, and after filling it with purified water, I added a stem of exotic red orchids. The earth element in the southwest was a miniature red tea-pot that I had purchased at a home store. I chose the metal teapot to symbolically represent the feeling of having form but remaining open to Divine inspiration. It also embodied the hot, abundant ideas that I imagined were ready to pour forth from a grounded place of practical inspiration deep within me. I placed an attractive red candle that looked like a bouquet of flowers for the fire element in the southeast. My Offering Tray was a copper plate. I then added red glass beads and a blank Angel Card®, on which I wrote the word *success* to stimulate what I wanted from this undertaking. Finally, I placed a Career and Recognition Necklace from my AltarWear® collection. It contained the Planetary Yantra and symbol for this direction, with stones and beads in the colors associated with the aspiration. I added a small statue of Ganesh in front of my Personal Symbol to remove all obstacles. I rested a very small picture of my spiritual teacher, Sri Sri Ravi Shankar, against my framed Personal Symbol. He had been my guide and anchor throughout this educational experience. His presence gave me inspiration and was a reminder that this journey had been a process of the heart, mind, and spirit. The completed altar was a joy to look at and represented my achievements. It reminded me to keep mind and heart open and my spiritual connections well tuned for whatever was next.

THE PLACEMENT

Air: A copper bell in the front right (northwest) quadrant of the altar.

Water: A small vase with water and orchids in the front left sector (northeast).

Earth: A teapot symbolizing a container holding new possibilities on the far right quadrant of the altar (southwest).

Fire: A red bouquet-shaped candle in the far left (southeast) corner.

Personal Symbol: A picture from my graduation with a small photo of my spiritual teacher resting on the frame.

Offering Tray: An Angel Card® placed in a copper dish in the center of the altar, containing red glass stones and a Career and Recognition Necklace.

Deity: The Hindu god Ganesh, known to support success in all undertakings.

Additional Items: Small gold paper stars sprinkled on the tray.

LAYOUT FOR CAREER AND RECOGNITION ALTAR

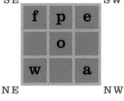

SUGGESTIONS FOR YOUR CAREER & RECOGNITION ALTAR

- Make sure the area is clean and your surface is against a south wall or window, or in the south sector of your home or office.

- The colors red and gold should be represented in some pieces on this altar.

- The water element in the northeast can be fresh flowers in the colors that correspond to the altar. You can use a vase that is clear or lightly colored.

- Add a red or gold candle in the southeast, or an oil lamp.

- Use stones or crystals in the southwest in red or golden colors. You can include a statue of Ganesh to remove all obstacles or Lakshmi, the goddess of abundance, a plant, or anything from nature.

- For the air element in the northwest, use a standing wind chime, incense, fan, or feather.

- Hang a red-colored Austrian leaded crystal on a red string in increments of nine inches over the center of your altar to keep the success and recognition you desire moving in your direction.

- Add a dish or small plate in the center of your altar to act as your Offering Tray. Use something in red or gold.

- To your Offering Tray add a Ganapati (Ganesh) Yantra to remove all obstacles to your success.

- On an unlined piece of paper that can easily fit onto the Offering Tray, add a handwritten word or some other symbolic representation of what you are requesting to receive from the Divine.

- Include a Personal Symbol in the center behind your Offering Tray. It can be a statue, photograph, collage, or picture that inspires feelings of success.

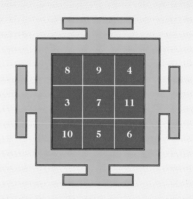

8	9	4
3	7	11
10	5	6

Each direction has a unique influence and a planet associated with it. The planet Mars influences career success and recognition and is associated with the south. If desired, you can use the specific directional yantra for Mars on your altar. You can sketch or trace your own version of the yantra, or go to our website at *www.vastucreations.com/freeyantras* for a free downloadable version you can use. Other activation processes can be found in Chapter Five. On the following page is the activation process for your Career and Recognition Altar, using the Mars Yantra and its corresponding mantra.

THE ACTIVATION CEREMONY

- Stand or kneel in front of your altar.

- Light any candle or incense that is on your altar. If you have bells or chimes on your altar, ring them to purify the energy in the environment. Their sound resonates with higher, subtle vibrations, bringing focused awareness to the present moment.

- Holding the Mars Yantra in your right hand, take ten to twelve long, slow, deep breaths in and out through the nose.

- Experience the feeling of having what you desire. Do not focus on specifics, just on feelings like happiness, peacefulness, fulfillment, love, and so forth.

- Place the yantra on the Offering Tray.

- With the right hand, extend the small (pinky) finger and your index finger, folding in the other two fingers against your palm, placing your thumb over the top of these two fingers to hold them in place. This a mudra, in Sanskrit, a hand position that moves energy in a specific pattern.

- With your hand in this mudra, facing the altar, move your arm forward and back nine times.

- Each time you extend your arm toward your altar you will say the following mantra with passion and intensity:
  Mantra: *Om Mangala Namaha*
  Phonetic pronunciation: Om Mon-ga-la Na-ma-haa

- Once you have completed this process, your altar is ignited.

- Take time each day to acknowledge it, even in small ways. This stimulates it and keeps it activated.

CORRESPONDENCES FOR THE CAREER & RECOGNITION ALTAR

PRIMARY COLOR	*Red*
SECONDARY COLOR	*Gold*
QUALITY	*Recognition*
AROMA	*Frankincense*
GEMSTONE	*Red coral, also red garnet, ruby, carnelian, or other red or golden colored stones*
METAL	*Copper, gold*
HINDU DEITIES	*Ganesh, remover of obstacles, Lakshmi, goddess of abundance*
YANTRA	*Ganesh Yantra**
MANTRA	*Om Gum Ganapataye Namaha* (pronounce Gum with an ng sound instead of an m)*
OTHER SPIRITUAL MENTORS	*Hermes, St. Caetanus, Archangels Michael and Chamuel*
PERSONAL SACRED ITEMS	*Awards, photographs, manuscripts, inspirational ideas that evoke the feelings of success*
SPECIAL PEOPLE	*Benefactors whose accomplishments you admire*
DAY OF THE WEEK	*Tuesday*
SOLAR SYSTEM	*Mars*
ANIMAL	*Lion*
LORDS OF THE DIRECTIONS	*Yama*
ELEMENT	*Earth/Fire*
PLANT	*Beech*
SENSE	*N/A*
SHAPE	*N/A*

*The Ganesh Yantra (with corresponding mantra) can be added to your Offering Tray or used as a separate or additional yantra to ignite your altar.

A Seeker of Divine Intervention

We have many clients who work in the computer industry throughout the world. Sanjeev had been at a large technology company for over a year and felt lost in the shuffle. He wanted more responsibility and more challenge, and though he enjoyed the team he was working with, he knew he had talents that were going unnoticed. Well trained to expand beyond programming, he wanted to move into management. With a sharp mind and a strong commitment to the company, he

> "The sound of chimes focuses the attention and brings the mind into present time."

was willing to do whatever was needed to create forward motion. He wanted some way of stimulating the change.

We went to see Sanjeev after he had moved into a new office, one with very little natural light. We helped him set up a Career and Recognition Altar and made a few Vastu adjustments to the room to encourage clearer thinking and productivity. The altar was placed on the south wall on a small table. As a base, Sanjeev used a red-colored scarf that belonged to his wife. We used a gold-colored vase as the water element, with a beautiful red rose to symbolize his passion for expansion. We placed a large dancing Ganesh in the southwest as the earth element. A dancing Ganesh is a symbol of overcoming obstacles with joy and is an excellent choice to represent career success. The fire element in the southeast, was a small gold candle in the shape of a star. For the air element in the northwest, we used a star wind chime. The sound of chimes focuses attention, brings the mind into present time, and stimulates the third eye, illuminating clear thinking. As a final addition, he added a pair of gold and ruby earrings he was going to give his wife for their anniversary. He wanted to energize them with the ceremony so they would be infused with his love and hopes for their future success.

Once ignited, Sanjeev's altar immediately began working wonders for his career. In a matter of months not only was he assigned to a more interesting team, he was given considerably more responsibility and a nice office with large windows. When he called to thank us, his voice was filled with gratitude.

Recreating Herself: A Mother's Story

A selection of items for a Career Altar

With her last child leaving for college, Laura began thinking about her own future. She had earned her degree in art some twenty years before. Since then she had raised three wonderful children. She had been a great mom but times were changing, and since her divorce she faced the necessity of finding a career

She decided to create an altar in the guest room in the south side of her home. She had set up her workshop there, and it seemed to be the ideal location for an altar dedicated to manifesting the career she had put on hold so long ago.

The act of assembling her altar was a profoundly meaningful experience. The altar became a statement of the genuine depth of her life journey. It offered her the opportunity to express her desires for the future while honoring the process that brought her to the door of new discoveries. Her Career and Recognition Altar connected her to the longings of her soul and to her creative force that had been channeled to others for so many years.

It was here she brought all of her hopes and also her fears of future success. It was here, sitting before her altar, that she developed a line of elegantly designed textiles that were a testament to her process and brought the career success she desired.

A Young Woman's Longing for Success

With her high school diploma in hand, Eve left home and headed for the big city. She wanted a different life than the one so many of her friends had opted for in the farming community of eastern Washington. She envisioned herself spreading her wings, but being a small town girl, she had fears of living and working in the big city. In her heart she knew if she didn't at least give it a try, she would regret it.

When we met, Eve had been working for a few months in a downtown coffeehouse and loving it. Her job was fast-paced and challenging. Every day new and interesting people came into her life, and some had become regular customers. Everything was going well, except that she was having difficulty making ends meet, even though she was sharing a small apartment. She wanted a way to let the Universe know she was open for something more. Within weeks after creating a

Career and Recognition Altar, Eve was offered more responsibility at work, promoted to site manager, and given a raise. She was overjoyed at how quickly results were obtained and was very grateful for the abundant generosity of the Divine.

Some choices of items for a Career Altar

Receiving Unlimited Grace

Support and assistance are always available to those who request help with an open heart and the willingness to learn and grow. Our life journey need not be one of loneliness, frustration, or separation from the comfort, kindness, and generosity that is ever-present through Universal Consciousness. It is possible to experience fulfillment in our chosen fields and become beacons to those who live in limitation and lack. There is a door opening for you. Walk through it and see what opportunities are waiting there.

"The true
way to render
ourselves happy
is to **love our
work** and
find in it our
pleasure."

—Francoise de Motteville

CHAPTER 9

Altars to Improve Health and Well-Being

Good health is a wonderful gift. It is a blessing to wake up in the morning feeling vibrant with energy, alert, positive, and ready for whatever work or activity you have planned. But some people get out of bed in the morning feeling tired and in pain, and whether physically or emotionally, they live with a certain amount of disability. They experience loss of sleep and are deprived of physical stamina or the clarity that comes from being fully rested. When you are not healthy, life can be challenging and difficult to enjoy. Poor health can be caused by a variety of factors. Some health challenges are caused by inappropriate life style choices. Without proper nutrition, exercise, and relaxation, you set yourself up for poor health. Other problems appear to be genetic in origin or caused by circumstances that seem beyond your control. Without good health, you view the world from a very different perspective than when your health is strong.

Healing on Many Levels

Russ lived in pain, the kind that would not go away. Multiple surgeries had left him house-bound, and countless doctors and prescriptions had not helped him heal. He had a brilliant mind but was trapped in a body filled with pain. Russ had become cynical and disappointed. Because of the pain, his temper was short and his ability to communicate with others was strained. He spent more and more time alone. What he needed most was a connection to others. It was his hardest life challenge – to need love and support but not to be able

to let it in. Russ's brother John called us to find out if there was anything we could suggest to help him. Russ had tried traditional medicine but it had not provided sufficient relief. His frustration and disillusionment were profoundly felt. It was the most difficult time of his life.

Having experienced my own share of physical hardship, I told John that along with extreme physical pain there was invariably an emotional component – one where the pain lived in the form of fear, grief, or lack of forgiveness. I suggested that working on the pain from a new angle might give Russ a vehicle to express the deep loss that was connected to his physical disability. I suggested John talk with Russ first and see if he would like us to help him build and ignite a Health and Well-Being Altar.

By the end of the day we heard back from John. Russ wanted our support. In fact, he was eager to see us as soon as we could arrange the time. I gave John a short overview of what we were going to do and made an appointment for the next morning.

Russ lived in a small, sunny apartment that was easy for him to move around in. He was an attractive man in his thirties, but the pain he lived with could be seen in his eyes. Before we arrived he had gathered several pieces that were meaningful to him to use on his altar.

There was a low table in front of an eastern window in his living room that was next to a comfortable chair where he spent time sitting every day. It was here we built the altar. We began with the air element. Russ had a wonderful carved wood hand with a piece of wire wrapped around the wrist. In it he placed some small bird feathers. The image evoked deep feelings and was quite symbolic for him: a willing, open hand, bound by an inflexible force yet desiring to fly free. For the water element, we put small orchids, ferns, and a white carnation into a clear vase filled with fresh water. In front of the vase he placed a few seashells gathered from trips to foreign lands. The earth element was a beautiful statue of Mother Mary who represented the love, compassion, and healing he so desperately wanted. To symbolize the fire element, we used a candle placed in a small gold plate that a friend had recently given him as a gift. The Offering Tray was a handsome octagonal mirror framed in gold, to which he added some mementos from happier times. An Angel Card® with the printed word *trust* was added. His Personal Symbol was a picture of himself out on the lake, sailing. He wanted to feel that unbounded freedom in his life again. In front of this, sitting on the mirror, he added a small statue of Ganesh, the elephant god, remover of obstacles. Russ resonated with the energy of Ganesh. He wanted to remove whatever obstacles stood in the way of

his healing and gain understanding about his situation. With this in mind, we ignited the altar using a Keystone.

We check in regularly to see how our clients are doing after we work with them. Russ reported an amazing breakthrough and support from a new source. Over the few weeks since our visit, he began to realize how his anger and frustration had alienated the people in his life who cared about him the most. This was a big revelation. In the process of dealing with the physical pain, he had built up protective walls which had separated him from the love and caring he so desperately needed. He said he was still in pain, but instead of resisting it, he was beginning to accept it and entertain the notion that it was there to teach him something he needed to understand.

He also told me that a friend had brought over a Reiki healer, a person who is trained in the laying-on of hands. This woman's healing ability was impressive, and through her gentle ways, over several sessions, she helped Russ remove some of the tension and apprehension that so many people who live in chronic pain experience. It was from these healings that Russ was able to feel moments of decreased pain, which for him was a miracle in itself. He became aware of inner peace for the first time in years, and waves of gratitude swept into his heart. From this place, by loosening the grip of futility, Russ began to embrace a world of new possibilities.

THE PLACEMENT

Air: A carved hand made of wood bound by a piece of wire with a feather in it in the front left (northwest) quadrant of the altar.

Water: A glass vase with orchids, a carnation, and a fern in water, in the far left sector (northeast).

Earth: A statue of Mother Mary symbolizing compassion and healing for Russ on the front right quadrant of the altar (southwest).

Fire: A candle in a small gold plate on the far right (southeast) corner.

Personal Symbol: A nicely framed picture of Russ sailing on the lake.

Offering Tray: Mementos placed on a gold-framed hexagonal mirror at the center of the altar.

Deity: Ganesh, the remover of obstacles and the god of wisdom.

Additional Items: A Keystone was used to ignite the altar and was placed in the Offering Tray along with his treasured personal artifacts. Extra water element — seashells.

LAYOUT FOR THE HEALTH AND WELL-BEING ALTAR

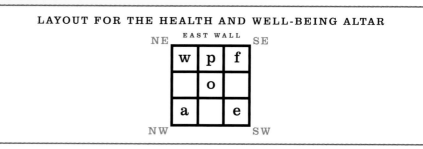

SUGGESTIONS FOR YOUR
HEALTH & WELL-BEING ALTAR

- Make sure the area is clean and your surface is against an east wall or window, or in the east sector of your home or office.

- The colors white and gold should be represented in some pieces on this altar.

- The water element in the northeast can be fresh flowers in the colors that correspond to the altar. You can use a vase that is clear or lightly colored.

- Use a white or gold candle in the southeast, or an oil lamp.

- Add stones or crystals in the southwest in white or golden colors. You can use a statue of the Medicine Buddha for healing, or one of Ganesh to remove all obstacles. You can also use a potted plant or something else from nature.

- For the air element in the northwest, use a standing wind chime, incense, fan, or feather.

- You can hang a clear Austrian leaded crystal on a red string in increments of nine inches over the center of your altar to keep the health and healing you desire moving in your direction.

- Add a dish or small plate in the center of your altar to act as your Offering Tray. Use something in the colors white or gold.

- Add to your Offering Tray a Mrityunjaya Yantra to help with health challenges. Or you can add a Ganapati (Ganesh) Yantra to remove all obstacles to the health and healing of yourself or others.

- On an unlined piece of paper that can easily fit onto the Offering Tray, write a word or phrase that evokes the feeling you would like to experience. You can also add other symbolic representations, such as Medicine Cards® or a tarot card.

- Include a Personal Symbol in the center at the rear of your altar. It can be a statue, photograph, collage, or picture that inspires feelings of health and wellness.

Activation Ceremony
Creating Health and Well-Being Using the Sun Yantra and Mantra

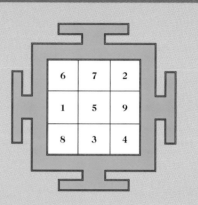

6	7	2
1	5	9
8	3	4

Each direction has a different influence and planet associated with it. The Sun influences health and is associated with the east. If desired, you can use the specific directional yantra for the sun shown in the diagram above. You can sketch or trace your own version of the yantra, or you can download a free version by going to our website at *www.vastu creations.com/freeyantras*. Other activation processes can be found in Chapter Five. On the following page is the activation process for your Health Altar, using the Sun Yantra and its corresponding mantra.

THE ACTIVATION CEREMONY

‖ Stand or kneel in front of your altar.

‖ Light any candle or incense that is on your altar. If you have bells or chimes on your altar, ring them to purify the energy in the environment. Their sound resonates with higher, subtle vibrations, bringing focused awareness to the present moment.

‖ Holding the Sun Yantra in your right hand, take ten to twelve long, slow, deep breaths in and out through the nose.

‖ Experience the feeling of having what you desire. Do not focus on specifics, just feelings like happiness, peacefulness, fulfillment, love, and so forth.

‖ Place the yantra on the Offering Tray.

‖ With your right hand, extend the small (pinky) finger and your index finger, folding in the other two fingers against your palm, placing your thumb over the top of these two fingers to hold them in place. This is a mudra, in Sanskrit, a hand position that moves energy in a specific pattern.

‖ With your hand in this mudra, facing the altar, move your arm forward and back nine times.

‖ Each time you extend your arm toward your altar you will say the following mantra with passion and intensity:
Mantra: *Om Surye Namaha*
Phonetic Pronounciation: Om Sir-yea Na-ma-haa

‖ Once you have completed this process, your altar is ignited.

‖ Take time each day to acknowledge it, even in small ways. This stimulates it and keeps it activated.

CORRESPONDENCES FOR THE HEALTH & WELL-BEING ALTAR

PRIMARY COLOR	*White*
SECONDARY COLOR	*Gold*
QUALITY	*Healing*
AROMA	*Lavendar*
GEMSTONE	*Ruby, red coral, red garnet, carnelian, or other red or golden colored stones, or clear quartz*
METAL	*Copper, gold*
HINDU DEITIES	*The Medicine Buddha, or Ganesh, remover of obstacles*
YANTRA	*Ganesh Yantra**
MANTRA	*Om Gum Ganapataye Namaha* (pronounce Gum with an ng sound instead of an m)*
OTHER SPIRITUAL MENTORS	*Apollo, Diana, Archangel Raphael, Nut — the Egyptian sky goddess, St Francis, Merlin*
PERSONAL SACRED ITEMS	*Pictures of yourself or others involved in enjoyable activities, items from times you experienced good health*
SPECIAL PEOPLE	*Those who have overcome their health challenges*
DAY OF THE WEEK	*Sunday*
SOLAR SYSTEM	*Sun*
ANIMAL	*Eagle*
LORDS OF THE DIRECTIONS	*Indra*
ELEMENT	*Ether/Fire*
PLANT	*Basil*
SENSE	*N/A*
SHAPE	*N/A*

*The Ganesh Yantra (and corresponding mantra) can be added to your Offering Tray or used as a separate or additional yantra to ignite your altar.

100

A Story of Faith and Courage

Amir and his wife, Maya, came to us to learn the breathing and meditation techniques we teach for the Art of Living Foundation. Maya's sister in Delhi had told her about the course, which is well-known in India, and said it would help them reduce the stress in their lives. When we met this couple, we did not know how much Amir was suffering from the effects of diabetes. Such a loving and gentle couple; over time they have turned into dear friends. During the first year we knew them, Amir's health began to decline. He had gone into the hospital for several surgeries related to the diabetes and was now on dialysis. It appeared that the surgery sites were constantly infected, and because of his waning strength he would spend much time in the hospital with high fevers.

Through all of this, Maya always looked on the bright side. She was so grateful for our phone calls of concern and support. We arranged to do some much-needed adjustments on their home, as well as building Amir a Health and Well-Being Altar. After balancing their home environment using Vastu Shastra, I instructed Amir to build an altar. It was placed on an antique wooden table against an eastern wall. When it was complete it was a well-designed, visual masterpiece, made with love and care. To ignite the altar, we used a Keystone. Instructing Amir to place it to his heart, I asked him to imagine a time in his youth when he was strong and lived with uncompromised health. He looked at me with eyes filled with tears, the emotion was so close to the sur-

The Sun influences health and is associated with the east.

An example of objects for a Health Altar

face. He then closed his eyes and followed the rest of my instructions, which included filling the Keystone with all this emotion, his hopes and dreams for an improvement to his compromised situation. Once the ignition was complete, he laid the Keystone in the Offering Tray on the altar. We hugged and he thanked us for what we had done.

Within a very short time, Amir's struggle with infection and hospital stays decreased. Many opportunities for possible transplants began appearing. Both he and Maya were very grateful for the help we had offered and thanked us many times for bringing them new hope and giving them the tools to help expand their perception of what was possible.

A Young Couple's Desire for New Life

Jerry and Jen, a young professional couple, wanted to start a family. They had been trying unsuccessfully for two years and were beginning to doubt their ability to conceive. They had even tried in vitro fertilization, with no luck. They were disheartened and skeptical. Jen's older sister had heard about us through a friend and insisted that she call us.

We talked about creating a Health and Well-Being Altar, and I advised her about a specific yantra we carry that helps with conception. We'd had some success using this yantra with other couples desiring children who had not been able to conceive easily.

Within three months of creating their altar, Jen and Jerry were happily pregnant and looking forward to a summer baby, whose expected birth date was on my birthday. Needless to say, the Divine works in mysterious ways!

An Altar for Man's Best Friend

Mac, a beautiful Black Labrador Retriever, was living with a degenerative liver disease, causing his family much worry and concern. It was hard to see him lying on the floor with no energy. His quality of life was being affected and his human parents did not want to lose him. They were willing to do whatever they could to keep him alive and bring him back to good health.

Items for a Health Altar

They put together a Health and Well-Being Altar, adding a very sweet looking, small statue of a dog as the Personal Symbol. Next an Angel Card® with the word *courage* printed on it and fresh flowers were added. They spent time in front of their altar sending out prayers for Divine intervention. Miraculously, over several months, Mac's health improved. A number of years have passed and he is still going strong.

The Source Provides

Creating an altar is a life-affirming act. Through altars, you are connecting with an unlimited power that can support you. When you or those you love experience health challenges, the simple act of creating this conduit to the wisdom of Divine Providence can give you comfort and solace. This in itself is a wonderful gift. In your own unique way, as you caringly select altar items that are meaningful, you create an on-going dialogue with these Universal Energies and open yourself up to their assistance. Within this field of unlimited potential, anything is possible.

> " These altars are designed as a sacred space where you can ask for Divine inspiration and grace to infuse your life and help make your dreams come true. "

"Look to your health; and if you have it, praise God, and value it next to a good conscience; for health is the second blessing that we mortals are capable of; a blessing that money cannot buy."

— Zaak Walton

CHAPTER 10

Altars that Heighten Spirituality

In recent years, more and more people in the western hemisphere have begun to create a personal spiritual connection with the Divine. This trend is noticed in everything from advertising to exercise. Twenty years ago, practices like yoga and meditation were considered to be on the fringe. Today they are very much a part of the mainstream and are offered in many places, including health clinics and hospitals throughout North America and Europe.

People are longing to experience spiritual growth and there are many accessible practices available to support a relationship with the Infinite that also positively affect body and mind. Taking time each day to do a simple practice creates harmony in our homes and in our lives. When we take this time and replenish our connection to that source of all possibilities, we become the peace we desire to find.

Practices such as meditation, Vedic breathing, and yoga will produce a strong nervous system and a calm mind. Your practice will be the safe harbor within the storm of changes that life can bring. An altar created for your spiritual growth can be the centering point to focus your connection with the Divine. Your practices and your altar go hand in hand. By bringing your body, mind, and spirit to your altar daily, you are honoring the power and grace that live within you.

Connecting with Spirit

I have done some form of meditation since the early 1970s, but it was not until I started practicing Vedic breathing and meditation that

I saw a significant change in my spiritual and emotional growth. Through these simple daily practices, my life transformed. Each day, I take time to sit in front of the altar designed specifically for my spiritual work and do my sadhana (a Sanskrit word for spiritual practice). By designing a Spirituality Altar, I established a place of silence where I could connect to the Divine. It is said that from this deep silence one experiences in meditation, magic happens. My life began to change in profound ways: my health improved, my relationships deepened, and I became more productive and effective. My life's work, which up until then had been so illusive, began to unfold. I was swimming in a river filled with new possibilities. With the stress removed as a by-product of this spiritual practice, I learned to relax and see where the river took me.

I placed my altar on a beautiful pedestal in our yoga room. For my water element, I choose a simple vase and added fresh, purified water and a beautiful stem of small orchids. Sitting in front of it was a small brass container of water. The air element was a brass incense burner to which I added incense with a sandalwood fragrance. Sandalwood is the aroma that enhances this aspiration. I chose a white candle for the fire element, placed in a copper plate, and also a small raised dish for camphor, which when burned has a purifying effect on the environment. I added a metal OM symbol on a stand for the earth element. OM is considered to be the primordial sound present in the Universe. The Offering Tray was round, made of brass, and because space was limited it contained my Personal Symbol — a beautiful brass and copper statue of Buddha placed toward the back of the tray. The plate also contained a crystal Shree Yantra which radiated its positive energy into the environment, and a necklace I designed called the Nine Planet Harmonizer, which has a balancing effect. It was placed on my altar when not being worn, to purify and charge it with supportive influences. A few pearls were added for some contrast and for decoration. To ignite this altar, a Keystone was used.

> " OM is considered to be the primordial sound present in the Universe. "

THE PLACEMENT

Air: An incense burner filled with sandalwood in the front left (northwest) quadrant of the altar.

Water: Orchids in a clear vase containing water in the far left sector (northeast).

Earth: A brass OM symbol in the front right quadrant of the altar (southwest).

Fire: A white-colored candle in a copper dish in the far right (southeast) corner.

Personal Symbol: A statue of the all-compassionate Buddha.

Offering Tray: Mementos placed in a round brass tray at the center of the altar.

Deity: Buddha, the compassionate one.

Additional Items: A crystal Shree Yantra was placed in the Offering Tray along with a Nine Planet Harmonizer Necklace from our AltarWear® line. A Keystone was used to ignite the altar.

LAYOUT FOR THE SPIRITUALITY ALTAR

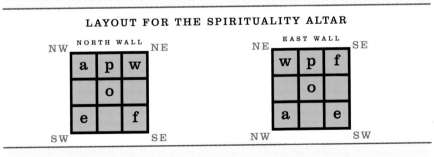

SUGGESTIONS FOR YOUR SPIRITUALITY ALTAR

- Make sure the area is clean and your surface is against a north or east wall or window, or in the northeast sector of your home or office.

- The colors gold and white should be represented in some pieces on this altar.

- The water element in the northeast can be fresh flowers in the colors that correspond with the altar. You can use a vase that is clear or lightly colored.

- Add a gold or white candle in the southeast, or an oil lamp.

- Use stones or crystals in the southwest in gold or white colors. You can add a statue of Shiva or Krishna to give you spiritual support. A potted plant or something else from nature can also be used.

- For the air element in the northwest, use a standing wind chime, incense, fan, or feather.

- You can hang a clear or gold-colored Austrian leaded crystal on a red string in increments of nine inches over the center of your altar to keep the spiritual connections you desire moving in your direction.

- Add a dish or small plate in the center of your altar to act as your Offering Tray. Use something that has gold or white in it.

- Add to your Offering Tray a Mrityunjaya Yantra to support your spiritual evolution and to destroy ignorance.

- On an unlined piece of paper that can easily fit onto the Offering Tray, write a word or phrase that evokes the feeling you would like to experience. You can also add other symbolic representations.

- Include a Personal Symbol in the center behind your Offering Tray. It can be a statue, photograph, collage, or picture that inspires your spiritual growth.

Activation Ceremony
Creating a Heightened Spiritual Connection Using the Jupiter Yantra and Mantra

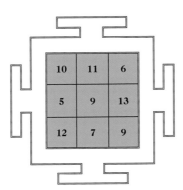

Each direction has a different influence and planet associated with it. Jupiter influences your spiritual connection and is associated with the northeast. If desired, you can use the specific directional yantra for Jupiter that is shown above. You can sketch or trace your own version of the yantra, or download a usable version by going to our website at *www. vastucreations.com/freeyantras*. Other activation processes can be found in Chapter Five. On the following page is the activation process for your Spirituality Altar, using the Jupiter Yantra and its corresponding mantra.

THE ACTIVATION CEREMONY

❋ Stand or kneel in front of your altar.

❋ Light any candle or incense that is on your altar. If you have bells or chimes, ring them to purify the energy in the environment. Their sound resonates with higher, subtle vibrations, bringing focused awareness to the present moment.

❋ Holding the Jupiter Yantra in your right hand, take ten to twelve long, slow, deep breaths in and out through the nose.

❋ Experience the feeling of having what you desire. Do not focus on specifics, just on feelings like happiness, peacefulness, fulfillment, love, and so forth.

❋ Place the yantra on the Offering Tray.

❋ Using your right hand, extend the small (pinky) finger and your index finger, folding in the other two fingers against your palm, placing your thumb over the top of these two fingers to hold them in place. This is a mudra, in Sanskrit, a hand position that moves energy in a specific pattern.

❋ With your hand in this mudra, facing the altar, move your arm forward and back nine times.

❋ Each time you extend your arm toward your altar you will say the following mantra with passion and intensity:
Mantra: *Om Brihaspataye Namaha*
Phonetic pronunciation: Om Bree-ha-spot-tay Na-ma-haa

❋ Once you have completed this process, your altar is ignited.

❋ Take time each day to acknowledge it, even in small ways. This stimulates the energy of your altar and keeps it activated.

CORRESPONDENCES
FOR SPIRITUALITY ALTAR

PRIMARY COLOR	*Gold*
SECONDARY COLOR	*White*
QUALITY	*Growth*
AROMA	*Sandalwood*
GEMSTONE	*Yellow sapphire or golden-colored stones*
METAL	*Silver, gold*
HINDU DEITIES	*Shiva, Krishna*
YANTRA	*Mrityunjaya Yantra**
MANTRA	*This is a complex, but extremely powerful mantra, which can be listened to on the homepage of www.vastucreations.com to learn the pronunciation. The words are* *Om tryambakam yajamahe* *Sugandhim pushti vardhanam* *Urvarukamiva bandhanat* *Mrityormukshiya maamritat*
OTHER SPIRITUAL MENTORS	*Vishnu, Archangel Uriel, Tara, Mother Mary, Isis, Kuan Yin, Jesus*
PERSONAL SACRED ITEMS	*Rosaries, malas, sacred religious symbols or items that bring a sense of closeness with the Divine*
SPECIAL PEOPLE	*Those who evoke a sense of divinity – a priest, rabbi, or someone you know who epitomizes a spiritual life*
DAY OF THE WEEK	*Thursday*
SOLAR SYSTEM	*Jupiter*
ANIMAL	*Rabbit*
LORDS OF THE DIRECTIONS	*Ishnaya*
ELEMENT	*Water*
PLANT	*Basil*
SHAPE	*Circle*
SENSE	*Taste*

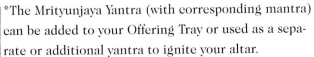

My life's work, which up until then had been so illusive, began to unfold. I was swimming in a river filled with new possibilities. With the stress removed as a by-product of this spiritual practice, I learned to relax and see where the river took me.

*The Mrityunjaya Yantra (with corresponding mantra) can be added to your Offering Tray or used as a separate or additional yantra to ignite your altar.

Honoring Spiritual Roots

Spirituality Altar items

Ming's family had been chased from their homeland in Southeast Asia many years ago during the darkest of times in a country torn by war. They had been a prosperous family, and lost everything as they fled for their lives. Separated from her parents and siblings, Ming ended up in an interim camp in Malaysia. It was three long years before her family even knew she was alive.

Ming, an industrious and courageous person, never forgot her deep connection to the spiritual forces that protected and guided her throughout her life. Always a bright, positive source of inspiration and kindness for others, she was a walking testament to what it means to keep your heart open and to live each day to the fullest.

After many years of dedication and hard work, Ming had become a superb chef by combining the Asian and French influences of her ethnic roots. She opened her own restaurant, which brought her success in the world and public acknowledgment for her unique contribution. Even with this success she never forgot to honor her connection to the Divine. She told me there had been many times she had been alone and felt like a stranger in a strange land. During those times she would call on Kuan Yin, the goddess of compassion and mercy, for love, support, and comfort.

Her work was her spiritual practice. Whatever she did, it was with loving kindness and a gracefulness that touched everyone around her. She created her Spirituality Altar at work. Using Kuan Yin as her Personal Symbol, she designed a beautiful altar that touched her heart. Ming always felt that whatever good came to her must come from the kindness of the gods. Her altar became a tribute to the love that had so graciously guided her.

The Blessing of a Spiritual Path

Sometimes it takes great loss for a person to let the Divine into their lives. This happened to Marla. Through some devastating events, she had lost the life she knew: her home, her children and the husband who had taken them all away. With very little left but her pride, she began to rebuild her life.

Items for a Spirituality Altar

When we met, Marla was beginning to recreate herself. She had come to an altars workshop to learn about creating a sacred place to pray and meditate every day. Even with all that had happened to her, she refused to blame, accuse, or feel like a victim. She had an inner strength and beauty about her that was inspiring.

After the workshop, Marla went home and created a simple altar following our instructions. She spent time before it daily, praying for healing. She wanted closure with the divorce so that she could find her way and be with her children again.

With the passage of several years, her life is quite different now. Although she never did regain custody of her children, she miraculously was able to maintain a wonderful relationship with them. Her guidance, caring, and love is evident in the way her children grew up. Marla is a beacon of light for many. Her kindness and genuine grace have deepened. She finds peace in her daily practice, giving thanks for the blessings in her life.

Michael's Altar

This chapter would not be complete without honoring my husband, Michael, and his sincere love and devotion to the Divine. He is a testament to what having an altar and a daily spiritual practice can be. Initiated at seventeen, he took to meditation and honoring a sacred lineage without hesitation. Michael has always had an altar set up for his personal work and to do puja (a ceremony used to purify the environment and, among other things, initiate people into meditation). After we developed the new altar layouts based on my research of Vastu Shastra, he changed his meditation altar to reflect the new format. He feels the layout used for the altars that are presented in this book encourages a successful, personal working relationship with Universal Energy.

Every morning at the crack of dawn you will find Michael in his meditation room sitting before his Spirituality Altar, covered in a silk shawl, doing his morning practices. To him there is no separation between the richness of his inner world and his daily life. He has become a light to so many by just being who he is: a simple man who loves God and his wife above all else.

> "Every morning at the crack of dawn you will find him in his meditation room sitting before his Spirituality Altar, covered in a silk shawl, doing his morning practices."

An Intimate Connection with Grace

Whatever you call God or Goddess or the All That Is, it is never far away. It is the whisper in your ear that speaks to you in quiet times. It is the miracle, the vision that you silently thank in your time of need. It is the comfort that you receive which inspires you to continue to reach for the sacred in your life. There is a power that offers universal peace which lives within the silence you so often resist. Within that peace is inspiration and the guidance that you have been longing for. Do not resist it; it has insight and influence to bring you your heart's desires.

114

"What lies behind us and what lies ahead of us are tiny matters compared to **what lives within us.**"

—Oliver Wendell Holmes

CHAPTER 11

Altars that Assist Life Changes and Transformation

There are times when you might be overcome by the enormity of changes that are occurring all around you. You may feel affected by situations or experiences that appear beyond your control. In trying times an altar becomes an oasis, a place of solace and refuge, where you can let go of your burdens and ask for the comfort and support you need.

Your life may be running smoothly, then something in your external world or your internal experience happens and your life is forever changed. You may be expected to keep your bearings during these times and even be called upon to be a support for others. Remaining balanced and strong can be a test for even the most centered person with a strong spiritual base.

During these challenging times it can be difficult to remember that you are lovingly supported in the Realm of the Unseen. You are never alone, even when you feel burdened, confused, hurt, or grieving. It is in reaching out and asking for support that healing and change can begin. When you are left with seemingly insurmountable problems, an altar for Life Changes and Transformation can bring you support and help align you with the All-Encompassing Presence.

A Soul's Life Lesson

Carly was unaware that she was sick. She wasn't experiencing any symptoms the day she went to the doctor for her annual check-up. The results of her exam appeared to worry her doctor. For several days she cried and waited to hear the results of the test he had run. At the

117

end of the visit the doctor had not been able to cover up the concern in his voice or in his eyes.

Carly's mind wandered to the darkest of thoughts. She believed in the concept of reincarnation and began to wonder, "If I were to die, have I fulfilled what I came here to do?" Five days can be a long time when a mind is in fear. It was a long time to worry about illness, death, and her future. I received a call from Carly on the third day of her wait. She was distraught and wanted a way to find peace in the midst of her pain and uncertainty. Because she lived in another state, I e-mailed her instructions on how to build a Life Changes and Transformation Altar designed to assist her in this difficult process.

Soon after receiving the e-mail, she built her altar and sat before it most of the day, praying and journaling. The next day she called to tell me that the process of building the altar had a most unusual and peaceful effect on her, and she now felt more at ease.

She had gone through her house and found items for the altar. She placed the altar on an east wall in the southeast area of her home, in front of an antique screen. Using a large silver tray on top of a low-lying table, she thoughtfully chose items for this very important altar. For the earth element in the southwest she used a conch shell decorated in silver. In the Vedic tradition, a conch shell is said to purify and transform the environment. It is a symbol of Lakshmi and brings good luck. To represent the air element in the northwest, she used silver metal cymbals, a gift from her yoga teacher. She had chosen them because their sound clears the mind. She used a bud vase with purified water and a sprig of cherry blossoms as her water element in the northeast. Carly's fire element in the southeast was a red candle with a floral pattern placed on a glass plate. For her Personal Symbol she chose a beautiful picture of a seated Ganesh, remover of obstacles and bringer of wisdom. The Offering Tray was an elegant silver-colored dish in which she placed red glass stones, a mala made out of sandalwood, a necklace of moonstone beads, and a heart-and-wings-shaped pin — a symbol of the Sufi tradition. She also added an Angel Card® with the word *surrender* printed on it. Coral beads and small crystal beads were used to decorate the tray. Igniting her altar with prayer, Carly asked the Divine Presence to support her and give her strength. She had decided to trust the process and knew she would remain open to the support she needed.

By day five, Carly was ready to speak to the doctor and hear about the lab results. The doctor was slightly embarrassed; the results were negative, a false alarm. Nothing was wrong, but she had changed. In the weeks that followed she began making different choices about her future and how she lived. No longer willing to wait for her life to take on meaning, she made active decisions that brought her spiritual growth and emotional rewards.

> " The altar had a most unusual and peaceful effect on her, and she now felt more at ease. "

THE PLACEMENT

Air: Beautiful silver cymbals in the front left (northwest) quadrant of the altar to clear the mind and purify the environment.

Water: A small bud vase filled with purified water and a sprig of cherry blossom in the far left sector (northeast).

Earth: A conch shell decorated with silver in the front right quadrant of the altar (southwest).

Fire: A red candle on a glass plate in the far right (southeast) corner.

Personal Symbol: A picture of Ganesh, the Hindu god who removes all obstacles and brings wisdom, in a beautiful silver frame.

Offering Tray: A mala in sandalwood and a necklace made of moonstone are placed over glass beads. Moonstone is good for women to wear, as it calms the mind and the emotions. The tray also contains a winged heart pin and an Angel Card® with the word *surrender* printed on it.

Deity: Ganesh, remover of obstacles.

Additional Items: Coral and red crystal beads are added to the silver tray for decoration.

LAYOUT FOR THE TRANSFORMATION ALTAR

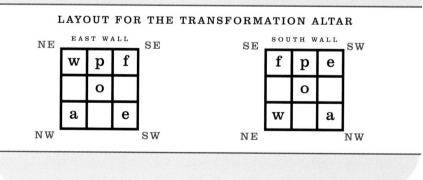

SUGGESTIONS FOR YOUR TRANSFORMATION ALTAR

- Make sure the area is clean and your surface is against an east or south wall or window, or in the southeast sector of your home or office.

- The colors silver and red should be represented in some pieces on this altar.

- The water element in the northeast can be fresh flowers in the colors that correspond to the altar. You can use a vase that is clear or lightly colored.

- Add a silver or red candle in the southeast, or an oil lamp.

- Use stones or crystals in the southwest in the colors silver or red. You can add a statue of Parvati to aid in life transitions, or Ganesh to remove all obstacles, a plant, or anything from nature.

- For the air element in the northwest, use a standing wind chime, incense, fan, or feather.

- Hang a red or clear Austrian leaded crystal on a red string in increments of nine inches over the center of your altar to support your desire for ease in this life change moving in your direction.

- Add a dish or small plate in the center of your altar to act as your Offering Tray. Use something in silver or red.

- To the Offering Tray add a Ganapati (Ganesh) Yantra to remove all obstacles to the transformation you desire.

- On an unlined piece of paper that can easily fit onto the Offering Tray, add a handwritten word, an AltarCard®, or some other symbolic representation of the feelings you request from the Divine.

- Include a Personal Symbol in the center behind your Offering Tray. It can be a statue, photograph, collage, or picture that inspires feelings of support and ease in transition.

Activation Ceremony
Support in Life Changes and Transformation Using the Venus Yantra and Mantra

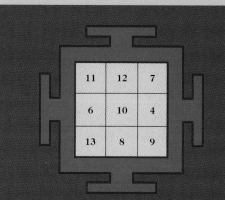

Each direction has a specific influence and a planet associated with it. The planet Venus influences the support you need for life changes and transformation and is associated with the southeast. If desired, you can use the specific directional yantra for Venus shown above. You can sketch or trace your own version of the yantra, or download a usable free version by going to our website at *www.vastucreations.com/free-yantras*. Other activation processes can be found in Chapter Five. On the following page is the activation process for the altar to assist you in Life Changes and Transformation using the Venus Yantra and its corresponding mantra.

THE ACTIVATION CEREMONY

- Stand or kneel in front of your altar.

- Light any candle or incense that is on your altar. If you have bells or chimes, ring them to purify the energy in the environment. Their sound resonates with higher, subtle vibrations, bringing focused awareness to the present moment.

- Holding the Jupiter Yantra in your right hand, take ten to twelve long, slow, deep breaths in and out through the nose.

- Experience the feeling of having what you desire. Do not focus on specifics, just on feelings like happiness, peacefulness, fulfillment, love, and so forth.

- Place the yantra on the Offering Tray.

- Using your right hand, extend the small (pinky) finger and your index finger, folding in the other two fingers against your palm, placing your thumb over the top of these two fingers to hold them in place. This is a mudra, in Sanskrit, a hand position that moves energy in a specific pattern.

- With your hand in this mudra, facing the altar, move your arm forward and back nine times.

- Each time you extend your arm toward your altar you will say the following mantra with passion and intensity:
  Mantra: *Om Shukraye Namaha*
  Phonetic pronunciation: Om Shu-kra-yea Na-ma-haa

- Once you have completed this process your altar is ignited.

- Take time each day to acknowledge it, even in small ways. This stimulates the energy of your altar and keeps it activated.

CORRESPONDENCES FOR THE LIFE CHANGES & TRANSFORMATION ALTAR

PRIMARY COLOR	*Silver*
SECONDARY COLOR	*Red*
QUALITY	*Transformation*
AROMA	*Myrtle*
GEMSTONE	*Diamond, colorless sapphire, zircon, clear quartz, white coral*
METAL	*Silver*
HINDU DEITIES	*Parvati, the Mother Goddess, and Ganesh, remover of obstacles*
YANTRA	*Ganesh Yantra**
MANTRA	*Om Gum Ganapataye Namaha* (pronounce Gum with an ng sound instead of an m)*
OTHER SPIRITUAL MENTORS	*Kali, Archangel Nathaniel, Libitina, Rinda, Mother Mary, Jesus*
PERSONAL SACRED ITEMS	*Objects that signify the desire for solace or support from the Divine*
SPECIAL PEOPLE	*Those who are an inspiration to you in this time of change*
DAY OF THE WEEK	*Friday*
SOLAR SYSTEM	*Venus*
ANIMAL	*Dove*
LORDS OF THE DIRECTIONS	*Agni*
ELEMENT	*Fire*
PLANT	*Mango*
SENSE	*Sight*
SHAPE	*Triangle*

*The Ganesh Yantra (with corresponding mantra) can be added to your Offering Tray or used as a separate or additional yantra to ignite your altar.

Honoring the Wisdom of Change

Juliet's husband Mark, a powerful man in his fifties, was suffering from the loss of employment. His work had afforded them a wonderful lifestyle and they were a very influential couple. Their long marriage had been filled with love, respect, and kindness for each other, their children, and their extended family. They were a charismatic team to say the least, and had been the strength and backbone of their community for years. To enter their home was to be immediately enveloped in their warmth and generosity.

It was a dark time for them. To be the ones in need of support and caring was a new role for Juliet and Mark. Living in these uncertain times was a humbling experience. Had it not been for Juliet's devotion to her personal growth and her willingness to see all transitions as doorways to greater good, this period of their lives could have been devastating.

Juliet called me for advice on what to do. I was traveling to their town the following week, so I suggested we put together a Life Changes and Transformation Altar for the members of the immediate family to use as a focal point for the transitions that were happening in their lives.

When I arrived, the whole family was there to participate in the process of igniting their altar. It was a moving and powerful testament to the kind of love that miracles are made of. Each family member offered items that were symbolic of their love for each other.

The situation did not get better immediately; they were in for some rocky times. It took months for Mark to find meaningful work, and in the process they made many adjustments. They honored the space for the change to occur, and until it was clear what their next step would be, they took time to meditate or pray in front of their altar. When things began to shift for the better, they were strong, united, and ready for what was next.

Changing Times, Changing Roles

An example of items for a Transformation Altar

Stella's family background had been associated with East Coast wealth and power, but she had opted for a more eclectic life than the rest of her relatives. Having moved away soon after college, her homecoming now, after so many years, was laced with many uncomfortable memories and unfinished business. Her parents were aging and in poor health, and it had fallen on her shoulders to help them. She felt awkward in her new role as caretaker. When she left, her parents had been strong and in good health. They were powerful people who moved in circles of great influence. She had not visited for many years and was shocked to see these once capable and very distinguished people in the state they were now in. Stella felt uncertain she would know how to manage their care.

She took our altars workshop prior to her move to the East Coast. She had the foresight to bring with her the makings of an altar to aid her in this time of adjustment and transition. Once set up and ignited, it brought her solace and granted her the time for contemplation and comfort. She found herself to be more than able to handle the affairs of the house and the care of her parents. Within this process of coming home, she healed the fears that had chased her away and those that had brought her back once again.

Become the Calm Within the Storm

Life is filled with uncertainties. Sometimes the more you attempt to control your world, the more difficult it is to find peace and resolution. When you are confronted with overwhelming burdens or find yourself afraid and pulling away, you must remember that miracles of life happen when the heart is open and you are fully engaged in every moment. Change is a certainty in life. It is how you choose to deal with it that is your greatest challenge and greatest gift. By living life with courage, your life transforms and the grace flows to you with ease.

"There can be no transformation of darkness into light and of apathy into movement without emotion."

—Carl Jung

CHAPTER 12

Altars to Increase Creativity and Knowledge

There is a creative force within you that is connected to the unlimited presence of the Universe.

This force is available to you for your uniquely personal creative expression. It is the gift that you are here to develop, the gift that feeds your individual growth and guides you to become a light for others. When you live in the present moment and open to this flow of creativity, you enter a new terrain and experience the timeless source of Divine Knowledge.

This flow of knowledge and creativity is available to everyone. By opening up to higher levels of consciousness through regular practices such as meditation, yoga, breathing, prayer, and honoring the sacred in your life, you finely tune the creative connections within your nervous system. It is through these practices that you tap into the resources available at the deeper levels of creativity. This is where true knowledge and profound individual brilliance reside.

Within you is the pathway to your unlimited creative uniqueness. By attuning to the more refined energies of Universal Wisdom, you move beyond limited, conditioned thought. This is the journey to the sacred within your home, your body, and your heart. If you allow it, it will fill you with wonder.

Sourcing Passion

The canyons off the Pacific Coast Highway near Malibu can be bitter cold at night, and this January night was no exception. Zoey pulled the coat up around her as she headed for her studio to finish the piece she had promised to deliver that week. A recent exhibition of her work had been well received, and she was beginning to make a name for herself in the local art community. With success sitting so close to the surface, it appeared she was doing well in her chosen field. The problem, Zoey believed, was not her lack of promise. There was something inside her that she was struggling to bring out: a passion and individuality that she felt she hadn't tapped into. This struggle to find her unique voice made it difficult to sleep at night. During the process of completing each painting, she was filled with constant doubt about her abilities. When she was young, she had experienced excitement and delight when she painted. She had lost those feelings over time by trying to maintain good grades in school and producing work that would be acceptable to others. The process of becoming a working artist left her feeling incomplete within herself. She wanted to source that place where confidence about her personal expression overflowed onto the canvas. She wanted to be the conduit for unbounded creative energy. Above all else she wanted to find that place, deep in her soul, that transformed her art into genius.

I met Zoey at one of our altar workshops in the Los Angeles area. She was intent on understanding everything that was being presented. During the break she asked me if I would be available to come to her studio and help her build a Creativity and Knowledge Altar. We agreed on a time to meet the following afternoon.

The drive down Pacific Coast Highway was beautiful. When I arrived at her small cottage off the main road that wound deeply into the canyon, she took me to the converted garage that served as her studio. Showing me her work, she spoke of her frustration in finding the well of inspiration and joy she wanted to convey. I asked her to sit with me for a few minutes in silence before we began designing the altar. In the workshop we had talked about how a spiritual practice was not only supportive for the success of any altar you make, but also for personal growth. Zoey had never connected to the world of Spirit except through her art.

For her, this first attempt to quiet her mind was exhilarating and difficult at the same time. An untrained mind can wreak

> There was something inside her that she was struggling to bring out: a passion and individuality that she felt she hadn't tapped into.

havoc on our daily lives, as we try to control our creativity, our purpose, and our life. I suggested, as a way to infuse the altar with power, that she find time every day to sit in front of it, to pray, chant, or meditate. We talked about her finding a daily spiritual practice that would strengthen her connection to her inner guidance. While there are many books on breathing practices, meditation, and yoga, it is a wonderful gift to have a qualified teacher initiate you into a practice. I told her of the great results I had obtained from the Art of Living practices, and left her the number for a local teacher. She agreed that having a spiritual practice was a missing piece for her and promised to explore the possibilities available.

That wintry afternoon Zoey and I created a beautiful altar. She chose an attractive antique table that her been her mother's, as a place to put her altar. For the water element in the northeast, she chose a blue crystal vase and filled it with small yellow orchids and delicate ferns. For her air element in the northwest, she hung a blue "flying lady" that she had purchased at an art gallery near her home. Within her was the desire to find freedom in her creativity, and she loved the expansive feeling this piece gave her. The fire element in the southeast was a small blue candle in a blue dish that she had found at the grocery store. She chose a statue of Krishna as her earth element. Krishna repre-

sented her need to express her creativity in a more playful way. The Offering Tray was blue glass. Within it she added a small collage that her niece had created at school, a blue stone necklace, and some pearls, which can symbolize a love of the fine arts and also intuition. She also added an Angel Card® with the word *creativity* printed on it, and a clear crystal ball to help boost the energy of her intent. For her Personal Symbol she used a large blue ceramic plate with a school of fish painted on it. To Zoey, the fish represented her desire for an abundance of new ideas and good luck, moving swiftly in a current of inspiration. For decoration she added a small book of sayings from wonderful women she admired. She also added a single silk daffodil. She wanted the creativity within her blooming as enthusiastically as daffodils do in the early spring. Finally, we ignited the altar with a Saraswati Yantra she had purchased at our altar workshop.

The entire process left a lasting impression on Zoey. She e-mailed me the next month that she had taken the breathing course from the teacher I had referred her to and had learned the mantra-based meditation practice that had been offered. She committed to taking time every morning to sit in front of her altar to pray, meditate, and breathe. It was her desire to access that spark of brilliance she longed for. Zoey mentioned that this commitment to herself was helping her feel more authentic in her art. She noticed she was spending less time caught in self-doubt, which freed up more energy to create. Her artwork was taking on a new quality, one that was unique and surprising. It had been a long time since she had enjoyed her creativity in this way. It was as if life was taking on a new dimension. She felt encouraged and excited to explore the vibrancy that was moving through her and displaying itself in her painting.

THE PLACEMENT

Air: A blue "flying lady" mobile in the far right (northwest) quadrant of the altar representing creative freedom.

Water: A blue vase containing small yellow orchids in water in the front right sector (northeast).

Earth: A statue of Krishna symbolizing the playful creativity she desired placed in the far left quadrant of the altar (southwest).

Fire: A blue-colored candle in small ceramic dish from a grocery store in the front left (southeast) corner.

Personal Symbol: A large blue plate with a school of fish swimming with the current, symbolic of the creative flow Zoey desired, in back of the Offering Tray.

Offering Tray: Mementos placed in a blue glass dish at the center of the altar.

Deity: Krishna, the god of joy and happiness.

Additional Items: A small book called *The Goddess Within*, a copper Saraswati Yantra, and treasured personal artifacts.

LAYOUT FOR THE CREATIVITY & KNOWLEDGE ALTAR

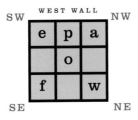

SW   WEST WALL   NW

e	p	a
	o	
f		w

SE   NE

SUGGESTIONS FOR YOUR CREATIVITY & KNOWLEDGE ALTAR

- Make sure the area is clean and your surface is against a west wall or window, or in the west sector of your home or office.

- The colors blue and yellow should be represented in some pieces on this altar.

- The water element in the northeast can be fresh flowers in the colors that correspond with the altar. You can use a vase that is clear or lightly colored.

- Use a blue or yellow candle in the southeast, or an oil lamp.

- For the earth element, add stones or crystals in the southwest in blue or yellow colors. You can use a statue of Saraswati, the Hindu goddess of creativity and knowledge, or Ganesh, the god of wisdom, to support your creative or educational pursuits. You can also include a potted plant or something else from nature.

- For the air element in the northwest, add a standing wind chime, incense, fan, or feather.

- You can hang a blue-colored Austrian leaded crystal on a red string in increments of nine inches over the center of your altar to stimulate the knowledge and creativity you desire moving in your direction.

- Add a dish or small plate in the center of your altar for your Offering Tray. Use something with blue or yellow on it.

- Add to your Offering Tray a Saraswati Yantra to enhance your creativity and knowledge.

- On an unlined piece of paper that can easily fit onto the Offering Tray, write a word or phrase that evokes the feeling you would like to experience. You can also add other symbolic representations, such as an Angel®, wisdom, or tarot card.

- Include a Personal Symbol in the center at the back of your altar. It can be a statue, photograph, collage, or picture that inspires your creativity and knowledge.

Activation Ceremony
For Increased Creativity and Knowledge Using the Saturn Yantra and Mantra

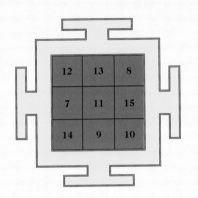

Each direction has a unique influence and planet associated with it. Saturn influences your spiritual connection and is associated with the west. If desired, you can use the specific directional yantra for Saturn shown above. You can sketch or trace your own version of the yantra, or you can download a usable version by going to our website at *www.vastucreations. com/freeyantras.* Other activation processes can be found in Chapter Five. On the following page is the activation process for your Creativity and Knowledge Altar, using the Saturn Yantra and its corresponding mantra.

THE ACTIVATION CEREMONY

❖ Stand or kneel in front of your altar.

❖ Light any candle or incense that is on your altar. If you have bells or chimes on your altar, ring them to purify the energy in the environment. Their sound resonates with higher, subtle vibrations, bringing focused awareness to the present moment.

❖ Holding the Saturn Yantra in your right hand, take ten to twelve long, slow, deep breaths in and out through the nose

❖ Experience the feeling of having what you desire. Do not focus on specifics, just feelings like happiness, peacefulness, fulfillment, love, and so forth.

❖ Place the yantra on the Offering Tray.

❖ With your right hand, extend the small (pinky) finger and your index finger, folding in the other two fingers against your palm, placing your thumb over the top of these two fingers to hold them in place. This a mudra, in Sanskrit, a hand position that moves energy in a specific pattern.

❖ With your hand in this mudra, facing the altar, move your arm forward and back nine times.

❖ Each time you extend your arm toward your altar you will say the following mantra with passion and intensity:
Mantra: *Om Shaniye Namaha*
Phonetic Pronunciation: Om Shawn-e-a Na-ma-haa

❖ Once you have completed this process, your altar is ignited.

❖ Take time each day to acknowledge it, even in small ways. This stimulates the energy of your altar and keeps it activated.

CORRESPONDENCES FOR CREATIVITY AND KNOWLEDGE ALTAR

PRIMARY COLOR	*Blue*
SECONDARY COLOR	*Yellow*
QUALITY	*Creative*
AROMA	*Eucalyptus*
GEMSTONE	*Blue sapphire, lapis lazuli, or any blue colored stones*
METAL	*Silver, bronze, or iron*
HINDU DEITIES	*Saraswati, goddess of knowledge and creativity, and Ganesh, the god of wisdom*
YANTRA	*Saraswati Yantra**
MANTRA	*Om Ayim Shrim Hrim Saraswati Devyai Namah – A pronunciation of this and other mantras are available at www.vastucreations.com*
OTHER SPIRITUAL MENTORS	*Ganesh, Archangels Gabriel, Michael, Uriel and Zedkiel, Minerva, Athena, and Hathor*
PERSONAL SACRED ITEMS	*Items that inspire creativity or heighten your desire for deeper levels of knowledge*
SPECIAL PEOPLE	*Artists, writers, teachers, those who inspire you*
DAY OF THE WEEK	*Saturday*
SOLAR SYSTEM	*Saturn*
ANIMAL	*Snake*
LORDS OF THE DIRECTIONS	*Varuna*
ELEMENT	*Air/Earth*
PLANT	*Eucalyptus*
SENSE	*N/A*
SHAPE	*N/A*

*The Saraswati Yantra (with corresponding mantra) can be added to your Offering Tray or used as a separate or additional yantra to ignite your altar.

Jamal was eloquent and had a way of communicating about life that was refreshing. A compassionate young man in his thirties, he had climbed the corporate ladder and was doing excellent work for the magazine where he was employed. His articles were informative and insightful, and the subject matter interesting to the magazine's readership. His challenge was not writing the articles, it was finishing the novel he had begun three years before.

Deep in his heart Jamal wanted to write full-time on his novel, yet he lacked the confidence and the commitment to do so. When we first met, he told me the book would be finished that year. Two years passed and he was no closer to completion. His inability to commit to writing at home had turned the book into a burden filled with neglected promises and feelings of disappointment.

Our next meeting was at the end of a beautiful Seattle summer. We met outside on the patio of a small city bistro, a wonderful sanctuary filled with overflowing baskets of flowers. By now, Jamal's frustration had become his daily mantra. He was embarrassed at his lack of progress. It appeared that the book had become, for him, a symbol of self-defeat.

> **His fears and disappointment dropped away as the writing poured out of him. The future seemed hopeful and filled with success.**

What Jamal lacked was a larger vision of his life. When he talked about the future, he had no real sense of what he wanted. His connection to his inner creative drive and inspiration was blocked. We talked about constructing a Creativity and Knowledge Altar as a way to tap into the Infinite Field of All Possibilities for his support. This excited him, and I happily gave him the instructions. I suggested that he assemble the altar and spend time before it regularly in contemplation, asking the Divine for guidance.

Jamal's altar was a beacon of inspiration. He placed his small creation on a tray on top of a round table in his home office. As he began to write, the wall of resistance built from all his frustration and negative thinking seemed to shatter. His fears and disappointment dropped away as the writing poured out of him. The future seemed hopeful and filled with success.

Wisdom from a New Perspective

Elise, a Feng Shui practitioner from the Midwest, put together a Creativity and Knowledge Altar to connect with the creative forces she wished to bring through her design practice. She felt that the teachings of Vastu Shastra would offer her new insights and deeper understanding into the process of creating environmental harmony. Her altar was her way to bridge Vastu Shastra and

A variety of items for a Creativity Altar

Feng Shui. It gave her a focal point to draw in the deeper wisdom she desired and to expand and grow in her professional education.

Take a Deeper Look

Tap into the creative force of the Universe and open yourself to all it has to offer you. As you do, what will drop away are the outdated and limiting beliefs that block your individual truth and knowledge. You are more than you envision yourself to be: unlimited energy, magnificent, unbounded creativity, wisdom, and compassion. Now is the time to reveal these gifts to yourself and live your life with creative brilliance.

"In order to have a real relationship with our creativity, we must take the time and care to cultivate it." —Julia Cameron

CHAPTER  13

Altars to Attract Helpful People and Universal Support

henever you need assistance for new projects, for new ideas, or for expansion and growth, an altar will align you with Universal forces and bring you the help you need. This force is an ever growing and expanding consciousness, and you are a unique part of it. Your uniqueness is more than just your physical characteristics, it is the way you express your individuality; it is how you choose to participate in the dance of life.

Life is happening all around you. You may stand on the sidelines waiting for opportunities to present themselves, or you can dive in and immerse yourself in new possibilities. The choice is always yours. By experiencing new things, you will know what resonates and is in harmony with who you are. Your mind may question what you learn and try to limit the possibilities, but if you follow your heart it will lead you on the path of personal discovery and empowerment. It has been said that if your mind is 100 percent empty, your hands 100 percent active, and your heart 100 percent full, then there is no room for regret, hesitation, or doubt. With expectancy, trust, and an open heart, ask for the support you need to move beyond limitations.

Requesting Support

Rose looked at the applications to law school that lay on her bed. Almost twenty years old, she would be graduating from college with honors in the spring. Her desire was to attend law school. It was a daunting proposition for one so young. Although she was more than capable, she wanted someone to help her understand the complexities of applying for school.

She was looking for someone who had been through it and was now working in the field of law and enjoying it. Rose had many questions about how to proceed and was at an impasse when she called me for information on how to build an altar.

As we talked, I asked Rose some specific questions about her situation and what she really wanted. I suggested she take some time to write down her doubts and concerns about finding the support she needed. The process would help empty her mind of the limiting thoughts and fears that energetically blocked her forward motion. Once this was done, she was to make a list of qualities representing her perfect mentor.

The next time we spoke, Rose had done her homework. She had felt overwhelmed, and writing down her concerns had given her mind a rest. Now she felt hopeful and excited about creating an altar to draw into her life the support she needed. By taking these actions she had alerted the Universe about her intention.

Creating the altar was a powerful experience for her. Rose chose objects that resonated with her goal. She placed a decorative runner on a favorite antique table in front of a window in the southwest area of her apartment. For the water element in the northeast, she used a crystal vase and placed in it a single red rose and a few sprigs of eucalyptus. In the southeast, she used a red candle in a brass container as her fire element. She chose a Chinese dragon to represent the earth element in the southwest. It is said that dragons possess the ability to foretell the future and are positive allies. She chose wind chimes as her air element in the northwest. The Offering Tray was a brass bowl. Within it she added glass beads, gold paper stars, and a copper Karla Siddhi Yantra to give her success in all her endeavors. Her Personal Symbol was a statue of Nataraj, the Cosmic Dancer who is the destroyer of ignorance and the overseer of the Universe. She placed this small brass statue of Nataraj on the base of a lovely Chinese fan. Both the fan and the statue were very complementary. Once all was complete, she lit the candle, rung the chimes and ignited the altar using the Rahu Planetary Yantra and mantra. Rose was profoundly moved; she felt her altar was a portal to success.

> **By taking these actions, she had alerted the Universe about her intention.**

THE PLACEMENT

Air: Wind chimes in the far right (northwest) quadrant of the altar.

Water: A crystal vase and a single red rose with eucalyptus in the front right sector (northeast).

Earth: A Chinese dragon as a support for her future goals on the far left quadrant of the altar (southwest).

Fire: A red candle in a brass container on the front left (southeast) corner.

Personal Symbol: A small statue of Nataraj, the Cosmic Dancer, on a stand holding a beautiful Chinese fan.

Offering Tray: Mementos placed in a brass dish at the center of the altar.

Deity: Nataraj, the Hindu god known as the Lord of the Dance, overseer of the Universe and destroyer of ignorance.

Additional Items: A Karla Siddhi copper yantra for success in all endeavors and a Rahu Planetary Yantra used to ignite the altar.

LAYOUT FOR THE HELPFUL PEOPLE AND UNIVERSAL SUPPORT ALTAR

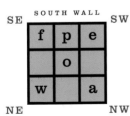

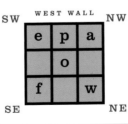

SUGGESTIONS FOR YOUR TRANSFORMATION ALTAR

- Make sure the area is clean and your surface is against a south or west wall or window, or in the southwest sector of your home or office.

- The colors orange and red should be represented in some pieces on this altar.

- The water element in the northeast can be fresh flowers in the colors that correspond to the altar. You can use a vase that is clear or lightly colored.

- Add an orange or red candle in the southeast, or an oil lamp.

- Use stones or crystals in the southwest in orange or red colors. You can add a statue of Nataraj, Lord of the Dance of Life, to give you support. You can also include a potted plant or something else from nature.

- For the air element in the northwest, use a standing wind chime, incense, fan, or feather.

- You can hang a gold-colored Austrian leaded crystal on a red string in increments of nine inches over the center of your altar to attract Helpful People and Universal Support.

- Add a dish or small plate in the center of your altar to act as your Offering Tray. Use something that has orange or red in it.

- Add to your Offering Tray a Ganesh Yantra to remove any obstacles in receiving the help you desire and to give you the support of nature.

- On an unlined piece of paper that can easily fit onto the Offering Tray, write a word or phrase that evokes the feeling you would like to experience. You can also add other symbolic representations, such as an oracle or AltarCard®.

- Include a Personal Symbol in the center at the rear of your altar. It can be a statue, photograph, collage, or picture that inspires your desire for the support of helpful people in your life.

Activation Ceremony

For the Helpful People and Universal Support Altar Using the Rahu Yantra and Mantra

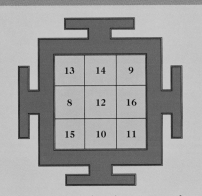

13	14	9
8	12	16
15	10	11

Each of the eight directions has a stellar influence associated with it. Rahu, the point of intersection between the orbit of the moon and the earth, influences the support you can receive from within yourself, others, and the Universe. Rahu is associated with the southwest. If desired, you can use the specific directional yantra for Rahu shown above. You can sketch or trace your own version of the yantra, or you can download a usable version by going to our website at *www.vastucreations. com/freeyantras*. Other activation processes can be found in Chapter Five. On the following page is the activation process for your altar to attract Helpful People and Universal Support, using the Rahu Yantra and its corresponding mantra.

THE ACTIVATION CEREMONY

- Stand or kneel in front of your altar.

- Light any candle or incense that is on your altar. If you have bells or chimes on your altar, ring them to purify the energy in the environment. Their sound resonates with higher, subtle vibrations, bringing focused awareness to the present moment.

- Holding the Rahu Yantra in your right hand, take ten to twelve long, slow, deep breaths in and out through the nose.

- Experience the feeling of having what you desire. Do not focus on specifics, just on feelings like happiness, peacefulness, fulfillment, love, and so forth.

- Place the yantra on the Offering Tray.

- With your right hand, extend the small (pinky) finger and your index finger; fold the other two fingers against your palm, placing your thumb over the top of these two fingers to hold them in place. This is a mudra, in Sanskrit, a hand position that moves energy in a specific pattern.

- With your hand in this mudra, facing the altar, move your arm forward and back nine times.

- Each time you extend your arm toward your altar you will say the following mantra with passion and intensity:
  Mantra: *Om Rahuaye Namaha*
  Phonetic pronunciation: Om Ra-who-aye Na-ma-haa

- Once you have completed this process, your altar is ignited.

- Take time each day to acknowledge it, even in small ways. This stimulates the energy of your altar and keeps it activated.

CORRESPONDENCES FOR THE HELPFUL PEOPLE & UNIVERSAL SUPPORT ALTAR

PRIMARY COLOR	*Orange*
SECONDARY COLOR	*Red*
QUALITY	*Stability*
AROMA	*Fir*
GEMSTONE	*Hessonite garnet, carnelian, or any other orange or red stones, amber*
METAL	*Lead*
HINDU DEITIES	*Nataraj, the Cosmic Dancer, Ganesh, remover of obstacles*
YANTRA	*Ganesh Yantra**
MANTRA	*Om Gum Ganapataye Namaha* (the m in gum is pronounced ng)*
OTHER SPIRITUAL MENTORS	*Archangel Michael, Mother Divine, Ceres, Horus*
PERSONAL SACRED ITEMS	*Symbols or items that inspire and bring a sense of support*
SPECIAL PEOPLE	*Family or friends, influential people, spiritual mentors or leaders*
DAY OF THE WEEK	*Saturday*
SOLAR SYSTEM	*Rahu*
ANIMAL	*Dog*
LORDS OF THE DIRECTIONS	*Niruti*
ELEMENT	*Earth*
PLANT	*Fir*
SHAPE	*Square*
SENSE	*Smell*

*The Ganesh Yantra (with corresponding mantra) can be added to your Offering Tray or used as a separate or additional yantra to ignite your altar.

> The Universe opened itself and her heart overflowed with gratitude for its abundant grace.

Creating Empowerment

A small group was gathering at my home to create a service project for the less fortunate in our community. Before they arrived I built a Helpful People and Universal Support Altar to enhance our meeting.

Since this was a very personal contribution to the group of volunteers, I did not mention the altar to the others who attended. I arranged the pieces with care. My intention was strong: to open us to a greater vision of creating community and to weave together our strengths in support of others. When I ignited it, I felt a palpable electrical current.

Once the meeting began my husband, Michael, led us in a short meditation to align our energies so that our meeting would be productive. I sent a small silent prayer to the altar, hoping to harmonize our energies. My vision was to bring in assistance from the Divine and to open our hearts to the support we needed to create something new and exciting.

Ideas began to flow and the energy between us was potent. We developed a project to empower underprivileged women in our community that was a balance between the heart, mind, and spirit. We named it The Empowerment Project. Once birthed, the project evolved rapidly. Doors opened and resources of people, funding, and

technology presented themselves. The project became a model for humanitarian work and community involvement worldwide.

Creating intention by building an altar can support a business as well as an individual. When you call on the unlimited power of the Universe, the conduit for you to receive assistance opens. A Helpful People and Universal Support Altar can also be your ally for serving others in your work and community. By being of service, you open yourself to the path of kindness and compassion. Your heart will become full and you will be blessed as a messenger of grace.

Universal Assistance

Many people come to our workshops on altars and Vastu Shastra looking for a way to connect directly with Universal Support for the purpose of creating meaningful change in their lives. Naomi had a comfortable job and felt happy to work in the field she loved, but she wanted to make an impact in a larger way. To do so she knew she needed to expand her circle of influence, connect with people, and share her new vision. Being more of a giver, it wasn't an easy proposition for Naomi to ask for this help. She decided that it was her personal challenge to ask for what she wanted and to be open to receiving it. She created her altar with the intention of requesting support from people and the Divine.

She spent time in front of her altar regularly. The process of taking time for herself in

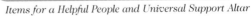

Items for a Helpful People and Universal Support Altar

contemplation gave her confidence that her contribution was a service that others truly needed. Very soon opportunities began to appear. She was overjoyed with the acknowledgment she was receiving for the talents and abilities she had and at how many people were willing to help. The Universe opened itself and her heart overflowed with gratitude for its abundant grace.

You Are Never Alone

Open yourself to the support that permeates the Universe and trust that you will be heard. When you create an altar dedicated to Helpful People and Universal Support, whether for your own needs or for others, the Unlimited Presence of the Divine will hear you. The support and power that is available in each and every moment is waiting for you.

"Help yourself,
and Heaven will
help you."

—Jean de la Fontaine

Celebrate Life

Rejoice in the passages of life. Creating an altar to honor a special moment in time deepens the experience of the event. It is a way to honor the people involved through ceremony, and offers kindness and blessings that feed the heart. Weddings, baby showers, birthdays, and anniversaries are just a few of the occasions where altars can be created. Because of their transient nature, altars for special occasions can be placed anywhere, inside or out. It is important that you place the objects used in their right directions: NE for water, NW for air, SW for earth, SE for fire, the center for your space element, and your Personal Symbol placed behind the space element. (See diagram.) You may require a compass to make sure you are setting it up properly.

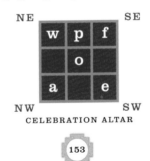

NE   SE

w	p	f
	o	
a		e

NW   SW

CELEBRATION ALTAR

<blockquote>
When you design an altar based on love, it will saturate the objects with wonderful blessings.
</blockquote>

A Time to Honor Union

Weddings — Start with pictures of the happy couple and add fresh flowers to your altar. Make sure that each of the elements is represented in its appropriate location as shown in the diagram.

Set aside time before the wedding day to create a ceremony that includes the altar. Give members of the family and/or wedding party cards to write notes to the bride and groom. These can be read aloud to them and then placed upon the altar. These words of wisdom, kindness, and joy can be used to ignite the altar and bring a unified, loving influence to the occasion. The altar will bring harmony for new beginnings. The blessings weave together those involved into a tapestry of loving support. Yellow and blue are colors that would be good to have on your altar, as they enhance love, happiness, and a successful union. Add some items in silver as well.

The Gift of New Life

Baby showers and birth celebrations — A delightful time to create altars is when new life comes into the world. Items that are appropriate to add to an altar dedicated to the birth of a child include baby shoes, building blocks, or a rubber duck. Make the altar part of the celebration. Notify the guests to bring small, meaningful items to add to the altar. Let them

Child's Creativity Altar

know that when they place the offering on the altar, you would like them to tell to the group why they chose their particular gift. This way, each item will come with a story and will have special meaning. When you design an altar based on love, it will saturate the objects with wonderful blessings.

Parents enjoy the process of making an altar at a baby shower or birth celebration, and have been known to use some of the items from the altar for their child's Creativity Altar when they are older. If you decide to transfer the items to a Creativity Altar for your child at a later time, place the new altar in the west to support the child. Use blue and yellow items, the colors of creativity, on this altar.

Life Is the Blessing

Birthday wishes — An altar to honor the passing year and celebrate the year to come is a wonderful gift for someone you love. Create an altar at a birthday party for another person, or make an altar to honor yourself on your own special day. Decorate the altar with candles and written blessings. Add items that touch the heart and inspire deeper feelings. When you design an altar created from love, it becomes a manifesting

meditation. Hold the desire for good health, success, and fulfillment in your heart when you assemble the altar. Those feelings will permeate the altar and bring blessings. Add white for health, red for success, and gold for fulfillment.

Items for an Anniversary Altar

Celebrate Every Moment

Anniversary blessings — An altar dedicated to celebrating an anniversary is a joy-filled and heartfelt gift. An altar built to commemorate two people dedicated to caring for one another and sharing their lives together is a wonderful act of tenderness and a way to honor their commitment. You can build an altar for an anniversary blessing to celebrate your parents' anniversary, your friends', or even your own. If you create this altar for your partner, place special items upon it that remind you of them. As part of the altar ceremony, let them know the significance of each of the items chosen. Placing your attention on loved ones through a carefully made altar is a genuine blessing. It honors them and the environment it is created in. It is an elixir that contains a healthy dose of love. Remember to add colors of yellow and blue to enhance the potency of this altar. You can also use items on your altar that signify a silver or gold anniversary.

> By creating an altar in celebration of yourself or others, you build a relationship with Divine Energy.

You Are the Blessing

In every way and every day, you are the blessing. The Divine reaches out and asks you to live your life fully within the richness that this present moment brings. Open your eyes and breathe deeply. Honor yourself and the Divine through acts of kindness. See your life as sacred. You are a part of the fabric of life, interconnected and relevant. To find joy and deep fulfillment, create a connection to the Eternal Presence that lives within you.

By creating an altar in celebration of yourself or others, you build a relationship with Divine Energy. Take time daily to sit before it and receive the blessings it will bring into your life. Trust the process. Have patience and know that you are heard and never forgotten. Honor your life. Your greatest gift is you.

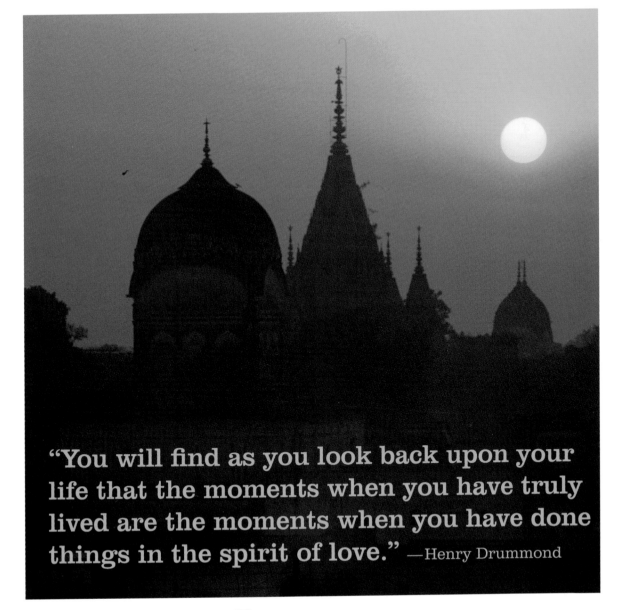

"You will find as you look back upon your life that the moments when you have truly lived are the moments when you have done things in the spirit of love." —Henry Drummond

CHAPTER 15

The Global Peace Altar

An Altar for World Peace

We gathered to pray for peace. Thirty women and men, old friends and new, came together at our home in Seattle to focus on a shared intention. For the occasion, everyone brought an object that held personal meaning to place on an altar.

It was April 30, and the moon was full. On this evening in many Eastern countries the festival of Wesak is celebrated in commemoration of Buddha's birthday. Some believe it is the anniversary of a legendary meeting of Christ and Buddha in a hidden Himalayan valley, and consider it a very auspicious time to connect with powerful spiritual energy. We felt it was a perfect opportunity for us to harmonize with others and ask for the blessing of peace.

The day before the gathering we built a three-tiered altar of wood in the open space under the central skylight in the living room. In a house designed according to Vastu principles, this location is called the Brahmastha-na, or center of awareness, and is the central point of a Vedic home where energy collects and comes into the house as a blessing.

We covered the altar with a white cloth. On the top tier we placed an empty bowl representing the space element to collect grace. At the four corners we placed items to signify the four directions — earth, air, fire, and water. On the second tier we placed figures of Buddha and Christ, along with candles and flowers. On the bottom tier

we arranged our pantheon of Hindu gods and goddesses and reserved space for guests to place their items. As guests arrived, we enjoyed a buffet dinner and spent an hour arranging and rearranging the ever-changing altar to achieve a sense of balance and harmony. Everyone got into the spirit of the evening and contributed their ideas as well as their sacred objects.

The end product turned out to be a remarkable assemblage of statues and pictures from spiritual traditions worldwide, arranged on the third tier and on the floor beneath it. Angels stood next to Krishna and Lakshmi; well-known Hindu deities and a laughing Buddha were placed around the corner from Mother Teresa. Guests arranged statues of Kuan Yin, the Chinese goddess of compassion, St. Joseph, the protector of families, and Our Lady of Guadeloupe, who brought a message of peace to beleaguered Mexican Indians after the Spanish conquest. Hanuman, the Hindu monkey god who protects against injury and helps in time of sorrow, peered out over a ceremonial Native American flute.

After dinner we lit the candles and incense, turned down the lights, and joined hands in a circle around our altar to quietly meditate. Then each of us told why our offering symbolized peace.

Kathleen brought a picture of the Wheel of Time Mandala, the Dalai Lama's personal peace symbol that Tibetan monks recreate as a sand painting when peace is threatened. Krista placed a picture on the altar of her mother, the family peacemaker, in a small heart-shaped frame. Joanne brought a tiny cuttlefish egg sac symbolizing the precious fragility of life. Several participants brought flowers: roses because

we are all flowers in God's heart; two Asian lilies on one stalk to signify the basic oneness of all humanity. Shelley brought a lush bouquet of white tulips with four sparklers inserted to remind us that humor is important, even in times of chaos, and Eric brought three enormous artichokes that symbolized the thorny problems we go through before we find the beauty at the heart of things.

Several people had contributed beautiful rocks from ashrams, churches, and other holy places where they had felt peaceful. Others brought photos of spiritual teachers who taught them to seek serenity. Jane added a lovely ceramic urn filled with spring water, which symbolized clarity for her. Sheila brought a traditional crystal bear carved by Native Americans to invoke the helpful power of the spirit world. Remy contributed a hand-painted gourd, a gift from a friend who wanted only to share his generous spirit.

As we listened to one another, our hearts seemed to merge and our spirits were uplifted in delight. We all laughed the laugh of recognition when Michael, who had built the basic altar from scrap lumber he'd found along the roadside, mentioned that focus and intention made the difference between seeing junk and realizing possibilities.

Focus and intention made the difference between seeing junk and realizing possibilities.

Together we had created not only a beautiful altar but also a warm sense of community that nurtured and supported our hopes for peace on Earth. It reinforced our belief that creating an altar and enlivening it with prayer, meditation, or ritual is a powerful way to focus intention and to bring in Divine grace.

It is a very powerful statement to build an altar to honor peace in the world, to create community and bring awareness to the intrinsic nature of all things. When you join together as one mind and one heart, you have great power. You can celebrate world peace on any full moon, the Wesak Moon, the Harvest Moon, or World Peace Day. Other times to honor Mother Earth are at the change of the seasons – such as the Vernal and Autumnal Equinoxes. These are all times when the energy is ripe to manifest our hearts' desires through Universal blessings.

A three-tiered altar is easy to build by using three boxes stacked one on top of the other and aligned parallel to the North-South axis. Tape the boxes together and then drape with a white sheet. Centered on the top box, place an Offering Tray or bowl. You can fill it with your desires written on small pieces of unlined paper or leave it empty for the Divine to fill for you. Add small items to represent the elements and place them on the top tier in the four corners, or if you use larger items, you can put the elements on the third tier down where there is more room.

The water element will go in the northeast corner, the fire element is placed in the southeast corner, the earth element will be in the southwest corner and the air element is placed in the northwest corner. The middle and third tier can contain symbols of peace, such as statues, pictures, offerings from nature, and words written on unlined pieces of paper. Flowers can be placed on each tier to add beauty, and large potted flowering plants can be arranged around the bottom of the altar. Boxes to create altars can be purchased or found at grocery stores.

Below are the dimensions of the boxes that can be used.
Top: 6"x 6"x 6" Middle: 16"x 16"x 16" Bottom: 24"x 24"x 24"

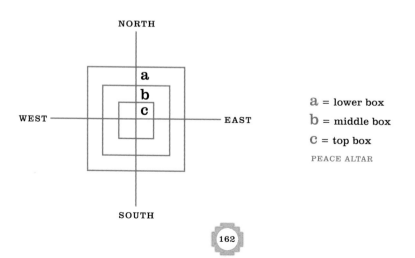

a = lower box
b = middle box
c = top box

PEACE ALTAR

"Peace between countries must rest on the solid foundation of love between individuals."

—Mahatma Gandhi

SECTION 3
Resources

APPENDIX I

Akasha – A Sanskrit word for space, ether, or the source from which everything manifests.

Air Element – Associated with the northwest, it is related to movement, change, and attraction.

Alchemy – The power to transform something into a much purer form.

Altar – A created structure or environment where ceremonies are performed.

Art of Living Foundation – An international humanitarian organization focused on service to others.

Aspiration – A desire to achieve something.

Avatar – The descent of a deity to earth, and its incarnation as a human or animal.

Devotee – An ardent enthusiast or dedicated member of a spiritual group.

Deity – A God, Goddess, or other Divine Being.

Divine – Noun: that which is God, a god, or a goddess; the underlying creative and sustaining force in the universe. Verb: to learn or discover something by intuition or inspiration.

Divine Feminine – The female aspect of the underlying creative and sustaining energy in the universe.

Divinity – The quality associated with being God, a god, or a goddess.

Earth Element – Associated with the southwest, it is the grounding influence, strength, and support that comes from that direction.

Feng Shui – The Chinese interpretation of Vastu Shastra which was adapted to the cultural, climatic, and geographical concerns of the region.

Fire Element – Related to the southeast, it is the energy that ignites forward movement, change, and transformation.

Gamma Rays – Non-life-supporting sun rays that come from the west as the sun sets.

Grace – Elegance, beauty, infinite love, mercy, and goodwill shown to humankind.

Guru – A spiritual leader who is prominent and influential in a field and is revered and followed by others.

Infrared Rays – The portion of the invisible electromagnetic spectrum consisting of radiation that is non-life-supporting from noon to 6 p.m.

Jyotish Astrology – Jyotish means "all knowing eye of the Veda." It is the oldest form of astrology in the world and originated in India.

Keystone – Something on which other interrelated things depend. Also, a product designed by Vastu Creations that guarantees protection and success in all undertakings and contains a very powerful symbol of the sun used to ignite an altar.

Lunar Energy – The moon's influence on the earth and its inhabitants.

Magnetic Energy – A phenomenon of physical attraction created by a moving electrical charge or current.

Magnetic Field – A region of space surrounding a magnetized body or current-carrying circuit in which the resulting magnetic force can be detected.

Magnetic Pole – Either of the two regions on the Earth's surface near the geographic poles where the Earth's magnetic field is most intense.

Mala – A string of beads used for chanting that can be worn as a necklace. It holds the vibrational energy of the words chanted.

Mantra – A sacred word, chant, or sound that is repeated during meditation to facilitate spiritual power and transformation of consciousness.

Memento – An object given or kept as a reminder of or in memory of somebody or something.

Menorah – A ceremonial candleholder consisting of a central stem surrounded by eight curved branches, used in the Jewish tradition.

Mudra – A Sanskrit word for a hand position that moves energy in a specific pattern. In this book it is used to move energy through the body to ignite an altar.

Offering Tray – An open container such as a plate, bowl, or any flat object in which you can place symbols of your intention.

Personal Symbol – A statue, picture, collage, or photograph which evokes an emotion and which is used as part of the altar design described in this book.

Puja – A ceremony honoring the Divine, which uses chanting, prayers, and ritual offerings that symbolically represent the five elements.

Resonant – A deep and rich quality of sound that produces or increases a sympathetic vibration.

Rishis – A Sanskrit word for scholars or men of great knowledge.

Ritual – An established observance; a rite or ceremonial procedure.

Rosary Beads – A string of beads used in praying.

Sadhana – A Sanskrit word for spiritual practice.

Sahaj Samadhi Meditation – A mantra-based meditation technique taught by the Art of Living Foundation that assists in removing unwanted stress and emotions.

Sanskrit – An ancient Indic language that is the language of Hinduism and the Vedas and is the classical literary language of India.

Shakti – A Sanskrit word for the feminine power; the creative principle at work in the universe, typically associated with the feminine component of the Divine, often embodied as a goddess.

Shrine – A sacred place of worship associated with a holy person or event; a case or container for sacred relics; a ledge or alcove for a religious icon.

Solar Energy – Relating to or originating from the sun.

Solar Magnetic Grid – Solar and magnetic energy lines which cover the surface of the earth in a manner similar to longitude and latitude lines running from east to west and north to south. When we align ourselves with true north we are in harmony with nature.

Sudarshan Kriya – In Sanskrit, *su* means proper and *darshan* means vision; a wonderful breathing technique that purifies the mind, body, and spirit taught by the Art of Living Foundation.

Sufism – The inner, mystical, or psycho-spiritual dimension of Islam.

Systems Thinking – Expanding a viewpoint to take into account larger and larger numbers of interactions as a subject is being studied.

Thermal Energy – Heat generated from the sun which affects the earth and its inhabitants.

Transformation – A complete change, usually into something improved.

Ultraviolet Light – Electromagnetic radiation beyond the violet end of the visible light spectrum; a component of sunlight that makes exposed skin become darker and is beneficial to all life forms.

Universal Support – The all-pervading Presence within the Universe that encompasses All That Is. It is ageless and unchanging.

Vastu Creations – Products, services, and trainings dedicated to the art and science of Vastu Shastra.

Vastu Shastra – The seven to ten-thousand-year-old architectural science of environmental harmony developed in India.

Vedas – The oldest sacred writings of Hinduism, including psalms, incantations, hymns, and formulas of worship.

Vedic – Of or pertaining to the Vedas.

Vortex – An energy, force, or all-pervasive power that draws everything toward its center.

Water Element – Associated with the northeast, this element affects spiritual and material growth.

Whole Systems Design – A field of study taught through The Center for Creative Change at Antioch University. It is defined as a system design which brings together the creative tradition of design, the dynamics of systems thinking, and the integrative understanding of holism. It is a trans-disciplinary approach to reframing human challenges to bring into existence a desirable, sustainable future.

Yajña – An elaborate system of Vedic rituals passed down through the ages. The action of the ceremony harnesses the power of nature to fulfill the desires of an individual or group.

Yantra – Geometric patterns designed thousands of years ago that are encoded with sacred sound. Each design transmits powerful frequencies and holds cosmic energy designed to enhance our lives. There are many different designs, each one having a specific influence on the environment.

APPENDIX II
GODS, GODDESSES, AND RELIGIOUS DEITIES

Abundantia – A beautiful Roman goddess of success, prosperity, abundance, and good fortune. She is also considered to be a protector of savings, investments, and wealth.

Agni – Agni is one of the most important of the Vedic gods. He is the god of fire and messenger of the gods, the acceptor of sacrifice. Agni is in everyone's hearth, he is the vital spark of life, and so a part of him is in all living things.

Apollo – The Greek sun god who oversees prophecy, light, music, and healing. He is one of the original Olympian gods and goddesses. He is son of Zeus and twin brother of the goddess Artemis.

Archangel Gabriel – Gabriel's name means "God is my strength." Gabriel is the messenger angel and helps with creativity, fertility, and communication.

Archangel Michael – Michael's name means "He who is like God." His chief function is to rid the earth and its inhabitants of the toxins associated with fear.

Archangel Nathaniel – Nathaniel's name means "Gift of God." He is lord over the element of fire and transforms consciousness from the limited self to the Eternal Self by burning away misconceptions that would have us believe that we are separate from God's love.

Archangel Raphael – Raphael's name means "God heals." Raphael is the healer-guide for humans and animals. He assists in healing of the body, mind, and spirit.

Archangel Uriel – Uriel's name means "God's light." Uriel assists in alchemy, spiritual understanding, writing, and weather. Call on his influence often, as he helps us in making informed decisions.

Archangel Zadkiel – Zadkiel means "the righteous of God." He is the Archangel of mercy and compassion. He helps us to see the Divine light within ourselves and others.

Artemis – The Greek goddess of hunters, sister of Apollo. She is the goddess of the wilderness and fertility.

Athena – The Greek goddess of wisdom, war, the arts, industry, justice, and skill.

Brahma – In Hindu mythology, Brahma is the Creator. Brahma; Vishnu, the Preserver; and Shiva, the Destroyer, form the Trimurti, the image of the three great gods of Hinduism.

Buddha – The father and founder of the Buddhist religion, Buddha was said to have been an avatar of the great god Vishnu. He taught about detachment from suffering through the attainment of inner peace.

Ceres – The Roman goddess of agriculture, grain, and the love a mother bears for her children.

Christ – Jesus Christ, the Son of God in Christian belief, is one third of the Blessed Trinity, which comprises Himself, His Father, and the Holy Spirit. He was sent to Earth to atone for the sins of mankind and to teach love and acceptance.

Diana – The Roman goddess of nature, fertility, and childbirth. She is closely identified with the Greek goddess Artemis. Diana is also a moon-goddess.

Divine Mother, also known as Devi in the Hindu culture — Devi means "Goddess." The Divine Mother has many other names and forms, such as the warrior goddess Durga, the destructive Kali, and Parvati, the gentle mother of Ganesh, the elephant god.

Eros – The Greek god of love and sexual desire. He was also worshiped as a fertility god.

Ganesh – The Hindu elephant god who is the remover of obstacles and who bestows wisdom, prosperity, prudence, and learning.

Hathor – The supreme feminine goddess of ancient Egypt. Hathor is the goddess of love, beauty, joy, dance, and music. She helps bring soul-mates together, and aids in fertility and the rearing of children.

Hermes – The messenger of the gods, Hermes is the god of shepherds, land travel, merchants, oratory, literature, weights and measures, athletics, and thieves. He is known for cunning and shrewdness. He brings dreams and good fortune.

Hera – The queen of the Olympian deities, worshiped as the goddess of marriage and birth.

Horus – The Egyptian falcon-headed sun and sky god, representing strength and victory. Horus teaches us to see all people through the eyes of love.

Indra – In Vedic times, Indra was the supreme ruler of all the gods, who were known as Devas in Indian mythology. The Devas included the god of war and the god of thunder and storms. Indra was the greatest of all warriors and the strongest of all beings. He was the defender of the gods and of mankind against the forces of evil, and is associated with the east direction.

Ishnaya – The Hindu god of the northeast who influences valor and spirituality.

Isis – One of the most popular goddesses in Egypt, Isis was worshiped as the Divine mother-goddess; she is the moon goddess who embodies femininity, motherhood, magic, healing, and power.

Kali – The Hindu mother goddess, symbol of dissolution and destruction. Kali destroys ignorance, maintains the world order, and blesses and frees those who strive for knowledge of God.

Krishna – In Hinduism and Indian mythology, Krishna was the eighth avatar or reincarnation of the god Vishnu. One of the most popular Hindu gods, Krishna is the deliverer of joy and happiness. He brings blessings to all relationships, especially of the romantic nature, and assists in spiritual awakening.

Kuan Yin, also known as Quan Yin – She is the Chinese goddess of mercy, compassion, and protection, and a symbol of the love and grace of the Divine Feminine Energy. Her name means "she who hears prayers." She hears and answers every prayer sent her way. She is devoted to helping us open to our spiritual gifts, attain profound knowledge and enlightenment, and reduce world suffering. It is said that the mere utterance of her name affords guaranteed protection from harm.

Kubera – The Hindu god of wealth. He is associated with the north and is at home in this direction; Kubera influences abundance and prosperity.

Lakshmi – The Hindu goddess of wealth, beauty, and good fortune.

Libitina – The Roman goddess of death and of both physical and spiritual metamorphoses; she also represents the death of outmoded ideas.

Luna – The personified goddess of the moon. She embodies the fullness of loving emotions and enchantment.

Merlin – Enchanter, wizard, and prophet; advisor to King Arthur. A powerful magician, spiritual teacher, and psychic visionary, he assists with alchemy, divine magic, energy work, healing, prophecy, and divination.

Minerva – The Roman goddess of wisdom, medicine, the arts, science, trade, and war. She is the daughter of Jupiter.

Mother Mary – Mother of Jesus the Christ, called "the Queen of the Angels"; she is the most loving, patient, and kind of the ascended masters. Call on Mary for support with healing, help with children, and for mercy.

Nataraj – The Cosmic Dancer; lord of the dance of life. He controls order and movement of the universe and is the god of destruction, regeneration, and sexuality.

Niruti – The Vedic god of the southwest, Niruti is all about support. If there is inadequate support, obstacles will present themselves.

Nut – The Egyptian sky goddess, the personification of the sky and of the heavens. She is the barrier separating the forces of chaos from the ordered cosmos in this world. Her fingers and toes are believed to touch the four cardinal points or directions.

Parvati - The Mother Goddess who symbolizes goodness, purity, power, and strength. She is associated with faithful companionship and fertility, and is the mother of the elephant god, Ganesh.

Rinda – The goddess Rinda of German mythology represents winter struggling to suppress the spring, even as people sometimes fight new growth because they find the process uncomfortable. Rinda teaches us how important it is to accept personal transformation gracefully.

Shiva – The third deity of the Trimurti, the Hindu triad of great gods which includes Brahma and Vishnu. Shiva is called the Destroyer, but he also embodies the aspect of regeneration.

St. Francis of Assisi – St. Francis is the patron saint of animals.

St. Gaetanus – He is the patron saint of job seekers and unemployed people.

St. Valentine – The patron saint of couples, love, and happy marriages.

Tara – In Hindu mythology, Tara was an astral goddess whose name meant "star." As stars provide navigation for sailors and travelers, Tara helps us to travel smoothly and safely find our way, whether on a trip, in our spiritual journey, or during daily life.

Varuna – One of the most important of the Vedic gods. Varuna is the lord of the cosmos, the keeper of Divine order, the bringer of rain, and the enforcer of contracts. He is omnipotent and omniscient; he is responsible for the sun moving in the sky, for day and night staying separate, and for the earth keeping its form; he is present in every gathering and knows every thought. He is at home in the west where he reigns supreme.

Vayu – The Vedic deity of the wind. He is the energy of change and is at home in the northwest.

Vishnu – A major god in Hinduism and Indian mythology, he is thought of as the Preserver of the Universe. Along with Shiva and Brahma, he is one of the three deities of the Hindu triad of great gods, the Trimurti.

Yama – Yama is the god of death and time. He oversees the energy of the south, where he is at home.

Mantras are Sanskrit words that free the mind. They contain specific sounds that create change in body, mind and spirit. A yantra is a geometric design that embodies subtle energy, which affects the environment in which it is placed. You can hear the sound of mantras by going to *www.vastucreations.com* and clicking on the appropriate link in the menu bar. To see planetary yantras, go to *www.vastucreations.com/freeyantras*. Additional yantras are also available on our website.

MANTRAS	YANTRAS
Ganesh Mantra *Om Gum Ganapataye Namaha*	**Ganesh Yantra** Use this yantra in any direction, to support removal of obstacles in your life.
Jupiter Mantra *Om Brihaspataye Namaha*	**Jupiter Yantra** A yantra associated with the northeast. This yantra assists in creating a heightened spiritual connection.
Mars Mantra *Om Mangala Namaha*	**Mars Yantra** Use this yantra for improvement and protection in career and business. It is also good for assistance in the removal of bad habits. The Mars yantra is associated with the energy of the south.

Mercury Mantra *Om Budhaye Namaha*	**Mercury Yantra** Mercury is associated with the north. Use this yantra for increasing abundance.
Moon Mantra *Om Chandraye Namaha*	**Moon Yantra** This yantra increases attraction in relationships. The moon yantra is at home in the northwest.
Mrityunjaya Mantra *Om tryambakam yajamahe;* *Sugandhim pushti vardhana;* *Urvarukamiva bandhanat;* *Mrityormukshiya maamritat*	**MrityunjayaYantra** An excellent yantra to assist in healing. Use it in the east on a Health and Well-Being Altar.
Rahu Mantra *Om Rahuaye Namaha*	**Rahu Yantra** Used to bring support from helpful people and the Universe. This yantra can be used in the southwest.
Saraswati Mantra *Om Ayim Srim Hrim Saraswati Devyai Namaha*	**Saraswati Yantra** The Hindu goddess of creativity and knowledge. This yantra is good for musicians and writers, and assists in the removal of creative blocks. Use it in the west on a Creativity and Knowledge Altar.
Saturn Mantra *Om Shaniaye Namaha*	**Saturn Yantra** Similar to the Saraswati. Use it for creativity and to support education and knowledge.
Shree Lakshmi Mantra *Om Maha Lakshmaya Namaha*	**Shree Yantra** This yantra attracts abundance into your life and can be used on a Prosperity and Abundance Altar in the north.

Ganesh Mantra *Om Gum Ganapataye Namaha*	**Sri Karya Siddhi Yantra** Used to bring about fulfillment of your desires.
Sun Mantra *Om Surye Namaha*	**Sun Yantra** This yantra influences health and well-being, and can be used on an altar in the east.
Venus Mantra *Om Shukraye Namaha*	**Venus Yantra** Associated with transformation and life-changes, this yantra brings ease in the transitions of life.

APPENDIX IV

FURTHER INFORMATION AND REFERENCES

RECOMMENDED BOOKS

Beckman, Howard. *Mantras, Yantras & Fabulous Gems*. Balaji Publishing Company, 1996.

Chopra, Deepak. *Creating Affluence*. New World Library, 1993, San Rafael, CA.

Grudin, Robert. *The Grace of Great Things*. Houghton Mifflin Company, 1990, Boston, MA.

Hall, Cally. *Gem Stones*. Dorling Kindersley, 1994, London, England.

Huston, River. *The Goddess Within*. Running Press, 1999, Philadelphia, PA.

Kanitkar, Hemant and Cole, W. Owen. *Hinduism*. NTC Publishing Group, 1995, Lincolnwood, Il.

Ratna, Daivegna, Chawdhri, L.R.. *Practicals of Yantras*. Sagar Publications, 1998, New Delhi, India.

Seth, Kailash Nath and Chaturvedi, B.K.. *Gods and Goddesses of India*. Diamond Pocket Books (P) Ltd., 1998 New Delhi, India.

Telesco, Patricia. *365 Goddesses*. HarperCollins, 1998, New York.

Virtue, Ph,D., Doreen. *Archangels & Ascended Masters*. Hay House, 2003, Carlsbad, CA.

Zander, Rosamund Stone and Benjamin. *The Art of Possibility*. Harvard Business School Press, 2000, Boston, MA.

Additional books are available on Vastu Shastra. Visit your local bookstore or your online buying source.

Angelology – *www.steliart.com*   Website references to Angels and Arch-angels.

Antioch University – *www.antiochsea.edu*   Online contact for information about Whole Systems Design.

The Art of Living Foundation – *www.artofliving.org*   General information about courses, service projects, and a list of centers worldwide.

Conscious Talk Radio – *www.conscioustalk.net*   Inspirational and informative, a talk show based in Seattle, Washington, that can be accessed through the worldwide web.

Encyclopedia Mythica – *www.pantheon.org*   A good source of information on the deities of most cultures.

Logos Resource Pages – *www.logosresoucepages.org*   Christian interpretation of New Age definitions.

Mantras Online – *www.sanatansociety.org*   A source to listen to mantras online.

Patron Saints - Patronage Index – *www.catholicforum.com/saints* An informative source of reference materials on saints of the Catholic tradition.

Suraj Brand Incense – *www.capricornslair.com/stickincense.html* Suraj Mysore Sandal Bathy is the most exquisite-smelling incense we have come across.

The Empowerment Project – *www.artoflivingseattle.org/volunteer.htm.* A humanitarian project founded by the local Seattle chapter of the Art of Living Foundation, dedicated to the empowerment and upliftment of underprivileged individuals through the teaching of technological skills and stress reduction techniques.

The Nag Champa Company – *www.thenagchampacompany.com* Great-smelling incense that everyone loves.

The Sacred Feminine – *www.thesacredfeminine.com*   Beautiful candles available online.

Vastu mantras, yantras, and products – *www.vastucreations.com*
A source for consulting, workshops, altar products, and listening to mantras.

Vidya Foundation – *www.vidyafoundation.com*   A sponsorship program for assistance in spiritual growth through the use of mantras, yajñas, pujas, and Jyotish (Vedic) astrology.

www.ancientegypt.co.uk/gods - Gods and Goddesses of Egyptian mythology.

www.arches.uga.edu/-godlas/Sufism.html - Information on the doctrine of Sufism in Islam, its practice, history, etc.

www.catholicforum.com/saints - Excellent information on Catholic Saints.

www.fire-serpent.com/cards/mandala.html - Beautiful yantra cards.

www.karunamayi.org - A source for ceremonies, spiritual information, CDs of mantras.

www.novaroma.com - A source for information about gods and goddesses of classical Rome.

www.quoteland.com - Quotations on every topic, by every author.

www.sarahsarchangels.com - A resource of information on the Angelic realm.

www.sarenamannaircraft.com - The source for the "flying women" sculptures shown in some photographs in this book.

www.thinking.net - A resource for systems thinking.

www.wisdomquotes.com - Quotations to inspire and challenge.

ADDITIONAL PRODUCTS FOR ALTARS
Runes and Divination Cards Used on Altars

Blum, Ralph. *Runes and The Book of Runes*. 1982, St. Martin's Press, New York, NY.

Farber, Monte. *Karma Cards*. 1988, Penguin Books, New York, NY.

Hay, Louise. *Power of Thought Cards*. Hay House, 1999, Carlsbad, CA.

Hubbs, Juliet Jaffray & Monaco, Nora. *Celestial Wisdom Cards*. 1990, Harmony Books, New York, NY.

Palladini, David. *Aquarian Tarot*. 1970, Morgan Press, Hastings-on-Hudson, NY.

Sams, Jamie & Carson, David. *Medicine Cards©*. 1988, Bear & Company, Inc., Santa Fe, NM.

Spilsbury, Ariel & Bryner, Michael. *The Mayan Oracle*. 1992, Bear & Company, Inc., Santa Fe, NM.

Tyler, Kathy and Drake, Joy. *The Angel Cards® Book*. 1997, Narada Publications.

Wanless, James. *Voyager Tarot*. 1985, Merrill-West Publishing, Carmel, CA.

Young-Sowers, Meredith. *Angelic Messenger Cards*. 1993, Stillpoint Publishing, Walpole, NH.

(**Note:** *Some of these cards may be out of print, but might be worth searching for in used book stores, online, antique book shows, etc.*)

About the Authors

Robin Mastro is a Whole Systems Designer from Seattle, Washington. She has taught hundreds of people of all ages how to create sacred space in homes and offices, and helped clients design altars that are not only beautiful but also have the ability to transform their lives. After completing her undergraduate degree in Art from Mills College, she continued on to receive a masters in Whole Systems Design at Antioch University in Seattle.

As a student of Whole Systems Design, she traveled to Egypt and India where she studied ancient concepts of sacred space. In India in 1992, she began her study of Vastu Shastra, the ancient art and science of architectural placement. Robin is dedicated to demystifying the wisdom of ancient systems to enhance the reality of modern life.

Michael, a successful Seattle builder and award-winning architect, has designed and built thousands of homes and apartments and over twenty million square feet of commercial and retail space. A meditator for more than thirty-five years, he traveled extensively with the renowned spiritual teacher, Maharishi Mahesh Yogi. He was asked by the Maharishi to design spiritual centers throughout the world, and began working with the principles of Vastu Shastra, the ancient Vedic system of placement believed to precede and form the basis of the Chinese art of Feng Shui. He applied this knowledge to building living environments in harmony with nature. In the process, he became one of the leading Western experts on the art and science of Vastu Shastra. The first Microsoft building was built by Mike using the principles of Vastu.

Robin and Michael have taught workshops up and down the West Coast and across the United States and Europe. Their company, Vastu Creations, offers products and cutting-edge tools for creating subtle yet powerful changes to homes and offices by using the teachings of this Vedic science.

FOR FURTHER PRODUCT INFORMATION, WORKSHOP SCHEDULES, NEWSLETTER
SUBSCRIPTIONS, OR TO SET UP CONSULTATIONS WITH THE AUTHORS,

PLEASE CONTACT ROBIN AND MICHAEL MASTRO
THROUGH THE OFFICES OF VASTU CREATIONS

1521 36th Avenue South

Seattle, WA 98144

(206) 328-0122

Info@vastucreations.com

www.vastucreations.com

Balanced Books

ORDER FORM

Please note whether you are ordering this for yourself or as a gift.
We can insert a greeting with the order telling the recipient that
the book is a gift from you.

○ This order is for me   ○ This order is a gift

NAME: _____

ADDRESS: _____

CITY: _____ STATE: _____ ZIP: _____

TELEPHONE: _____

E-MAIL ADDRESS: _____

If this is a gift, please write down recipient's name: _____

Your order for **Altars of Power and Grace** (International shipping extra)

- _____ copies ($19.95 each) . . . . $ _____
- Sales tax, add 8.8% for books shipped to Washington State . . . . $ _____
- Shipping, $4.00 for first book and $2.00 per additional. . . . . $ _____
- Total enclosed. . . . . $ _____

PAYMENT OPTIONS   ○ Check   Credit Card: ○ Visa   ○ MasterCard

CARD NUMBER: _____

NAME ON CARD: _____ EXP. DATE: _____

SIGNATURE: _____

E-MAIL ORDERS: *orders@balancedbookspub.com*
TELEPHONE ORDERS: 206.328.3995 or 877.838.4858
FAX ORDERS: 206.328.1339
POSTAL ORDERS:
Balanced Books, P.O. Box 14957, Seattle, WA 98144

Please send more FREE information on

○ Other books   ○ Seminars   ○ Products   ○ Consulting   ○ Newsletter